For What May I Hope?

American University Studies

Series V
Philosophy

Vol. 104

PETER LANG
New York • Bern • Frankfurt am Main • Paris

Gene Fendt

For What May I Hope?

Thinking with Kant and Kierkegaard

PETER LANG
New York • Bern • Frankfurt am Main • Paris

Library of Congress Cataloging-in-Publication Data

Fendt, Gene
  For what may I hope? : thinking with Kant and
Kierkegaard / Gene Fendt.
    p. cm. − (American university studies. Series V,
Philosophy ; vol. 104)
  Includes bibliographical references and index.
  1. Hope.   2. Hope − Religious aspects − Christianity.
3. Kierkegaard, Søren, 1813-1855 − Contributions in
concept of hope.   4. Kant, Immanuel, 1724-1804 −
Contributions in concept of hope.   I. Title.   II. Series.
BD216.F46   1990   128 − dc20   90-40500
ISBN 0-8204-1387-9   CIP
ISSN 0739-6392

© Peter Lang Publishing, Inc., New York 1990

Printed in the United States of America.

How a book, this book in particular, comes to be is beyond me.
Nonetheless, I will be credited with it, for good or ill. No matter.

For the good in it there are others to thank, and so

to my teachers and fellow students, but especially to Maryanne
Bertram and James Robb, who introduced me to philosophy,

to Carl Fehring, Mark Siegchrist and Ulla Bruun de Neergaard,
who taught me words,

to Louis Mackey and Lars Gustafsson, who gave me enough rope,

to Therese, Mark and Mad, Monica, Steve, Emmet, Harvey, Tom,
Matt and Gale,

to the people who have taken up the only vocation more difficult and
more important than teaching, my parents,

and to one who shall remain nameless, *sine qua*—

this work has been dedicated in love and gratitude.

Acknowledgements

This text has gone through 4 computers and 3 word processing programs, and I have frequently been overmastered by the technology of these irreplaceable labor saving devices. However, thanks to the timely (sometimes at 2 in the morning) help of Earl Richards of the University of Texas Philosophy Department and (less early in the day) Steve Pitkin and David Clark of Kearney State College it has finally been wrested from the static void and put out here on paper. The quotations from Kant and Kierkegaard are with the permission of the respective publishers wherever they are not my own.

Quotations from Immanuel Kant's *Religion within the Limits of Reason Alone*, translated by Greene and Hudson (1960), are with the permission of Open Court Publishing, Peru, IL.

Quotation from Søren Kierkegaard's *Prefaces*, translated by William McDonald (1989), is with the permission of Florida State University Press, Tallahassee, FL.

Quotations from Immanuel Kant's *The Critique of Judgement*, translated by James Creed Meredith (1952), is with the permission of Oxford University Press, Oxford, England.

Quotations from *Kant's Critique of Pure Reason*, by Immanuel Kant, translated by Norman Kemp Smith are reprinted with permission of St. Martin's Press.

Table of Contents

Proem

Chapter 1: The Centrality of Hope

Chapter 2: Is Hope Reasonable?

Chapter 3: The Character of the Religious in Kierkegaard's Drama

Conclusion

PROEM

I: A Point of View for the Work of the Author

And how should I begin?
—T.S. Eliot

Vorrede, Vorwort / Forord / Forword, Forward

"This is a seduction. If you believe that you have
already succumbed, for that you believe him is just
what a seducer wants. If you do not believe it you are
in trouble, for it is a seduction. Not to believe that it is
a seduction makes it impossible ever to escape from
it. Believe it or disbelieve it, you will regret both. In
fact it is already too late to decide or even put off a
decision. The seduction has already succeeded. You
may as well go forward; you cannot go back."

This word should have stood as a warning at the top of Kierkegaard's authorship. That it did not stand there decides nothing
about the authorship. The warning would—as the warning with
which this book begins shows—accomplish nothing. Except,
perhaps, awaken "my dear reader" to the fact that she is—in
beginning—guilty. Such a warning would be useful *per exemplum*
to a writer who wished to begin with a dogmatic point about original
sin, but neither I, nor Immanuel Kant, nor, for that matter, Søren
Kierkegaard, lay claim to being writers of dogmatic theology.

Very well then, what are we? We have this in common: we (each
of us in his own way) began by allowing ourselves to be seduced. But
then, so did you, *kære læser*. After that things get rather cloudy.
And confusing. Except of course for Kant: he is the philosopher's

philosopher—the Touchstone of every critical theory, every metaphysic and epistemology and every ethical writer since his time. For the rest of us...

When I was a young graduate student in the little harbor town of Chicago I began to lust after Lady Philosophy. The other graduate students (whom I perceived as competitors) were very impressive. I was pretty sure I didn't have much of a chance. Indeed, occasionally I wondered why she had even beckoned me thither. A few of the other graduate students were like the ubiquitous gray snow—just there for six months of the year, lying about—but most were clear-eyed aspirants. They had very definite ideas about Philosophy and how to win her favors: They would make theses. And so they sat down and set about it with a definite style and force. I saw immediately that I was not able to accomplish much in that line, and if I could, it would never be quite so well formed as the definitive theses produced by those other aspirants. I decided that I would have to take a different tack. I would write "the decisive thesis on...." Somewhat later I saw that I could not even manage that much, but could at best work out "a decisive" one. Still, that would be different—perhaps even singularly so—and this difference might be enough to attract Philosophy's eye and bring me into her arms. There only remained to define a thesis. Or, rather, to decide on one. Since any work on theses is, after all, an act of hope, the thesis was decided: it would be on hope. In this way the form, content and act of writing it would all—I hoped—coincide. I hoped it would be a happy coincidence and result in a marriage. This, at any rate, was my proposal.

Since then, I have come to wonder,[1] hundreds of miles from any

large body of water, about theses. Can language hold a *thesis*,
contain it? Suppose that it can; must it not at the same time hold,
contain—or must it outlaw?—*arsis*: "the raising of the foot in
keeping time." "*Thesis*," that means, in the first place, "to put
one's foot down." Can a person approach Philosophy with only
theses, or do we not need an equal measure of *arsis*? Is Lady
Philosophy a lover of theses, or are such things so clumsily obtrusive
that they could not possibly win a woman's heart? Could a person
dance by only putting his foot down? I was tempted to say, aren't the
best dancers more arsis than thesis, but I suppose that depends on the
dance. In any case, a dancer must be equally adept at putting his
foot down as at lifting it up. There, I have put my foot down.

In more philosophical terms, what if "understanding and
interpretation are not thematic acts?"[2] Or again, what if there is
something prehensile about a thesis, some proto-repression in
assertion so that assertion is born out of violence, or at least with the
prophecy of violence binding it, as Oedipus—inescapably,
inescapable, inescaped. Would a wise woman marry a tragedy
waiting to happen?

Now it may be that Lady Philosophy—for that Philosophy, like
Truth, is a woman I have never been so skeptical as to question
(unlike writers like Nicolaus Notabene in his eighth "Preface")—it
may be that she has an answer for me. It may be that despite my
more polite nature she answers me as she did Nicolaus:

> "You are under a misapprehension. It has not been
> granted you to understand me. Yet you should not
> therefore be angry with me, for I am not the one who
> creates human kind. You are not capable of

comprehending me. I do not say this to offend you,
even if you were the only person who was too dense
for that; my quiet peaceful, blessed life offends no
one. But you are not the only one. What applies to
you applies to many others; indeed it applies to the
bulk of people, to which you belong. I am only for the
chosen, for those who are marked early, in their
cradle. And in order that these shall belong to me,
time and industry and opportunity are demanded,
enthusiastic love, the magnanimity to dare to love
hopelessly, renunciation of much that other people
consider beautiful, and which really is beautiful too.
The one in whom I find this, I reward also with the
kiss of the idea; I make the concept's embrace
fruitful for him. I show it to him in a far higher
world—there I let him understand and see how the
thoughts grow in one another more and more
copiously. That which is dispersed in the manifold
of languages, that which is everywhere present in the
speech of the most sagacious, is gathered here and
thrives in its quiet growth. I cannot show myself to
you; I cannot be loved by you. Do not think it is
because I am too proud. No! But my being entails it
like this. Goodbye! Do not demand the impossible.
Praise the gods that I exist, for even though you do not
comprehend my being, there are nevertheless those
who do comprehend it. Rejoice then that the fortunate
become fortunate. Do that and you will not regret it"
(*Prefaces*: 94).

But I am given to loving hopelessly—I would not, as it were, "say to her face that it is not her beauty, but only [my] advantage which attaches [me] to her" (*FMM*: 443)—and so such a response is, to me, the greatest encouragement. Still, where Nicolaus had the advantage of hearing the voice, I have not heard, nor ere seen the Lady, which makes my case all the more hopeless. Well. An empty space is place enough for love to move through.

So much for my hopes and secret aims. For Søren Åbye Kierkegaard things are more difficult to figure out. He gives us a "confession" of sorts, in fact he gives us several. It is helpful here to recover the original of this literary convention: St. Augustine confesses that for a long time he was an outsider to his own life. From that outside view his life is a shambles of incidents and rootless wanderings. But one of the changes that follows upon his conversion is an understanding that the shattered story of his times has a beginning and an end in eternity, a beginning and end that make it a narrative whole in which the incidentalia of his temporizing are given the significance of Eternity seeking him out. Understanding and confession first become possible, according to Augustine, after conversion. They first become possible together: to understand is also to confess. That the first "confession" of world literature came into existence after Christianity appeared could be taken as proof that at least some new thing became possible because of its appearance. Such an argument would, however, be a logical fallacy.

For Kierkegaard the metaphor is best modulated from time into space: Kierkegaard's corpus lies in Fragments, Postscripts, Speeches, Diapsalmata (*ad se ipsum*), Letters, Diaries, Discourses,

Sermons, Essays (in short, nearly every form that can be found in the history of philosophy) under his own name and names that are not his own, names that seem to say too much, names which keep silent and names that contradict each other, but like Augustine he confesses that there is a unity, created by Governance, in the shattered dissembling artifice that would be called by his name. He confesses, like Augustine, that he was led, seduced, sometimes forced, nearly always unaware: unity of his self is not the creation of the self because that self is not a pure *unum*. The self, he says, is a self in relation to God, the power which constitutes it; therefore it can be seen to be unified only by taking up that relation with all of the passion the self has (for that it is a relation is, as we shall see, the source of all its passion).

Should we believe such confessions? Among the things Kierkegaard confesses are that some of his writings are meant to entrap readers, seduce them. He admits further that they were successful. Too successful, for the readers of his day would not accept with their right hands what he gave with his right hand, but took with their right hands what he offered in the left. Most of his later interpreters have been more generous: they have graciously accepted in their right hands the religious works that Kierkegaard confesses to be humbly offering in his right hand.[3] Armed with his confession that the writer was first and always a religious author, they have made him into a pre-eminent religious writer, perhaps the pre-eminent religious writer of the age. Certainly all the books and articles signed "S. Kierkegaard"[4] do have explicitly religious themes or overt religious implications. This includes *The Point of View for my Work as an Author* which confesses that "the whole authorship is related to Christianity." I suppose the whole authorship must include also this sentence "in the pseudonymous works there is not a single word which is mine," which S. Kierkegaard published in "A First and Last Declaration" some two years before he wrote the *Point of View*.

There are no contradictions here—everything "S. Kierkegaard" wrote is "related to Christianity and the problem of becoming a Christian." That among the things he wrote were interpretations of works not signed by him and in which (by his own "first and [but not really] last declaration") there is not a single word that is his is nothing unusual. Nor is it unusual for a religious writer to interpret other works of literature in accordance with his "blick."[5] But in our own day S. Kierkegaard has gone further. He is credited also with some dozen or so more works than he signed. "Credit" is often assumed to be a logically transparent relation, despite the fact that it is an economic and ethical mystery. (Kant, for example, has tremendous problems with it in *Religion within the Limits of Reason Alone*). We are, however, not interested in its economic or ethical meaning, merely in its logic, and since credit is logically transparent—let us assume that credit is logically transparent—and so these 12 or so works, unsigned by Kierkegaard, are credited to him and thus credited with "having a relation to Christianity and the problem of becoming a Christian"... In this fashion a system of existence has become possible where before it was not so. In this system there are three so called "spheres of existence;" one moves between spheres via a leap; the leap is triggered by despair; only the third sphere can coherently and authentically avoid despair (which it does by virtue of the absurd);

the third sphere recovers (though it transcends) the immediacy which was in the beginning.[6] Et cetera. *Og således videre.* So runs the credo of the orthodox interpreters.

Indeed, he has so far exceeded in his death what he accomplished in his life that there are now town criers of his doctrine that "the truth is subjectivity." Or, what passes for the same thing, assistant professors hurrying to press with books and articles, would be paramours of philosophy with and without theses, explications of his concepts without irony, disciples of first and second degree. In short, what was once considered to be an impossibility, namely to paint Mars in the armor that made him invisible, now succeeds very well indeed.

Perhaps this is all a seduction. It is certainly comfortable. Scholarship has shown how each brick of the work fits into the cozy system of existence (*det hyggelige værtshus*) that S. Kierkegaard confesses he discovered (very nearly *ex post facto*) that he was living in.[7]

I have been taken with a different idea, a somewhat heretical point of view: The work is from first to last a work of seduction. The intention of the author in all of the works—those signed by S. Kierkegaard as well as those credited to him—was primarily seduction and secondarily ... seduction. This SÅK was no ordinary seducer, but among the great seducers, and of them the greatest. To possess a woman's body for a night is a poverty-stricken goal which, no matter how interestingly carried off, eventually ends. (As Johannes complains: "why can such nights not be longer"). SÅK was a seducer without peer, for his object was to possess a woman heart and soul both in time and in eternity. To succeed in this primary objective would be enough to make him first among storied seducers, but his secondary objective, also a seduction, puts him at the ideal apex of seductivity. His secondary objective was to have the whole story recorded and yet avoid discovery ... via seduction. He would draw his reader aside, whisper "this is all for religious purposes" and win the title "great religious thinker" for his activity. Which activity, I say again, was first and last a seduction.

This admittedly heretical theory has a historical point of departure. It first came to me in a general sort of way when a young lady (this was many years ago) who was the object of my fancy, as well as several lower affections, repulsed my advances in favor of those of another friend of mine who became a Jesuit. This unhappy accident first made me aware of the attractions of the religious life. A second historical accident made me reflect this rather general theory into the particular case of SÅK. Many celibate years after failing with the aforementioned object of my fancy, etc. I found a delightful little book entitled *Forlovelsen* which was published for Mrs. Regine Schlegel by Raphael Meyer in 1904. This, one may assume, is a straightforward little book by a simple honest woman. Along with Mrs. Schlegel's story Meyer published Kierkegaard's letters to her from the time of the engagement. Of these Meyer notes "the first 20 present nothing as a basis for dating; I have ordered them according to my best judgement with regard to the mood which prevails in them." Here Herr Meyer, unconsciously one must guess, follows somewhat the pattern "A" followed, who, having "received from Cordelia a collection of letters, whether it includes all of them I do not know" (letters similarly lacking dates), introduced them into his manuscript "where the motives seemed to suggest them" (*E/Or* I: 306-7). Among these there were several which echoed in feeling and mood, sometimes in exact expression, the letters which "A" discovered and published with the "Diary of the Seducer." Some of Kierkegaard's letters to Regina are, of course, echoed in other works. One may indeed well imagine that bits of SK's conversations with Regina—bits which only she would be able to recognize—abound in his works. Regina says as much:

> as newly engaged we see them sitting together in Schlegel's room reading Kierkegaard's writings aloud to each other. And they indeed contained one after another pieces of her past, memories from the time of the engagement, studies of him and her, works which by Kierkegaard's poetic genius were turned into *Dichtung und Wahrheit*. And these readings continued the whole of their youthful lives

according to Meyer.[8]

This, of course, was new only to me. The scholars have known it for quite some time. Almost fortuitously I came upon a passage in SK's diary. He had sent a letter to Herr Schlegel asking if a rapprochement would be possible and, if so, that he deliver an enclosed letter to his wife, Regina. Schlegel refused. In his diary Kierkegaard wrote angrily: "She may belong to him in time, but in eternity she is mine."[9]

If we put these two little pieces together we have the outline of the story of the greatest possible seduction of all time. What seducer ever won the heart and soul of a young girl from a man, and then, after casting her off, kept his words and spirit alive in her heart not only in spite of that man (who became her husband), but through that husband's own voice? There in Schlegel's own room, there in Schlegel's voice she was reminded again and again of her first love, of her own promises to her first love.[10]

That would be enough to make Kierkegaard the greatest of all seducers in a qualitative sense. He certainly cannot compete with 3001 in Spain, but—to make a merely grammatical point—quantity is the element of comparison, the superlative is purely qualitative, therefore I say again that this is the greatest of all seducers. But in addition (if it is possible to add to the superlative), Kierkegaard is also praised by the ethically and religiously minded critics. His love for Regina is said to be true; his dismissal of her a sacrifice to the religious. Regina's husband reads the story of his "sacrifice" of her—the world is enraptured. She hears her husband read a beautiful story, she understands it much better than the one delivering the message—she has heard the story before and it is about her—she is enraptured again.[11] The seducer says the story has religious significance, he names the main characters Abraham and Isaac—the world believes him. For the world it all has religious significance; Kierkegaard possesses her heart and mind even as Herr Schlegel drones on next to her on the couch. For the seducer, on the other hand, the dismissal is not a sacrifice but a requirement of the ideal. For without such a casting off the result would soon enough be marriage, by which the ideal is lost and reality forces its way in. Moreover, the dismissal is required most of all in the highest seduction, for a reflective seducer is well aware that a maiden "always tends to be loyal when the loved one wishes to be rid of her." "After all, a girl loves only once" (*E/Or* I: 373).

But this is altogether too demonic to be believed. All those

religious writings—a mere cover? Perhaps not merely cover. In all
of them there are almost certainly phrases Regina had heard
before, in other contexts. Later they are placed in the context of a
religious discourse—what could be further from seduction? Indeed,
what discourse could be further from the purpose of twining about her
heart than such remarks as "if it were true—as conceited shrewdness, proud of not being deceived, thinks—that one should believe
nothing which he cannot see by means of his physical eyes, then
first and foremost one ought to give up believing in love," a remark
which opens *Works of Love* (23)? Nothing could be further from the
spirit of seduction, unless of course, there might be another context
in which these words had been uttered. Something that might sound
like an echo *fra Drømmen af hendes Ungdomsvaar*. A modern
writer uncovers the scene of ravishment:

> Is the scene always visual? It can be aural, the frame
> can be linguistic: I can fall in love with *a sentence
> spoken to me*: and not only because it says something
> which manages to touch my desire, but because of its
> syntactical turn (framing), which will inhabit me
> *like a memory.*[12]

What if it were the case that "deception extends as far as the
truth, ... seduction, artifice and hypocrisy as far as love, equally as
far" (*WL: passim*)? As another writer has said because there is
discourse about faith, hope and love, and about God and Jesus Christ,
presented in a solemn tone ... it does not follow that it is godly
discourse by any means. What counts is the manner in which the
speaker and listener are related to the discourse, or are presumed to
be related (*CUPS*: 374n). Yet a third writer adds this warning: "And

devils soonest tempt, resembling spirits of light" (*LLL* IV,iii).

To carry this on throughout a life, through the Corsair affair, through the attack on the Church, would take a tremendous dedication to the ideal. But no one denies that Kierkegaard was capable of such "purity of heart." No one was more tenacious of the ideal. It doesn't seem to fit the mode of life described as aesthetic, which has no unity. But then perhaps that system of existence with the three spheres is a ploy, perhaps it is a seducer—The Seducer *par excellence*—who is saying the life of the aesthetic seducer is fragmented and can never be unified. In other words, perhaps that too is a lie, and the aesthetic life can (and in this case does) have a unifying principle. It is at least possible that the SÅK who wrote until the "religious experience" of 1848 was seducing the woman. But I prefer the stronger thesis: Think of the honor among his kind, the eternal delight, at having seduced the whole world as well as the woman. Perhaps even through the woman, for who could read Kierkegaard's works and not love Regina?

I hear an impatient interlocutor:

> But now to the result! Has [Kierkegaard] accepted
> Christianity or has he rejected it, has he defended it
> or has he attacked it? ... Verily, no maiden who has
> pledged herself and her love to silence[13] and be-
> comes immortal through keeping her pledge, no man
> who takes every explanation of his life with him to
> the grave, no one, no one could carry himself more
> circumspectly than _____, while achieving the still
> more difficult task of keeping silent through

speaking (*CUPS*: "Something about Lessing," 61).

Verily, Johannes Climacus seems to have it right, about somebody.

What was at the heart of this man? I would not say that this point of view on Kierkegaard's work as an author is true. The evidence I have elicited is only circumstantial. Any further evidence I could elicit would also be only circumstantial; I would not go to court with it. This makes the theory even more seductive, for if I could prove SÅK was a seducer his unmatchable crime would be less remarkable, imperfect. But as it is I cannot prove that he is a seducer, and the crime, if there was a crime, remains a perfect one. Nonetheless this point of view is possible, as, of course, is the religious point of view. If it is true, then the summary judgement upon SÅK's life and work would perhaps be something like this: "His life had been an attempt to realize the task of living poetically" (*E / Or* I: 300). Of course you may, like Regina's older sister, Cordelia, "believe all the same that he is a good man."[14] One's point of view depends upon a choice of the heart: Cordelia Wahl.

Concluding Unscientific Postscript to this Fragment

There is another possibility: It could be that *The Point of View* was really written by Johannes Climacus as a way of jibing at SK's pretensions in the note attached to JC's last book. For certainly JC would see it as pretentious that SK should disclaim responsibility for the words of "the pseudonyms" while at the same time claiming authorship of their works. For JC, who clearly knows that "the point of view of immanence exists only for contemplation, essentially and in truth only for God, and is an illusion for worshipful professors" (*CUPS*: 133), the highest joke that could be played on someone who pretentiously pronounces upon the freedom and responsibility of other individuals is to portray him as someone who pretends to have—essentially and in truth—the point of view of immanence, to portray him, in other words, as some Absolute Spirit who

> from the chalice of the realm of spirits
> foams forth for Him his own infinitude.[15]

This would require a consistent humorist—who could only be a moment in such an Absolute Spirit—to sign the book with the Absolute Spirit's name rather than his own—exactly what the invisible Johannes does by signing Kierkegaard's name to *The Point of View*. Such a play would trump Magister Kierkegaard absolutely, and would be sweet revenge for JC, who, every time he turned around, found that what he had intended to do was already finished in its truth by the good Magister.[16] Thus the ironical sublation of JC's merely imaginary authorship in Magister Kierkegaard's actual work would be finally and absolutely recovered by a work actualized by JC but imagined in the name of Kierkegaard and in fact actually "credited to" him. Johannes would in this way also reap his poetic justice upon philosophy: he began as a young student attempting to doubt everything, as philosophy commanded he begin; he would here end by making a whole authorship the logically necessary movement of a completely detached ironic ___. Of course, if J.C. did indeed do this we would have no evidence for it except the Logic which is outlined in this argument and the peculiar "prophecy concerning Esau and Jacob, that the greater was destined to serve the less" (*CUPS*: 241). This theory would make the entire authorship of Kierkegaard something that takes place and is spoken only in his absence, never when he is present (*CUPS*: 234), thus fulfilling S. Kierkegaard's oft reiterated wish about his texts, each of which "wishes only to be what it is, a superfluity, [desires] only to remain in retirement, as it was in concealment it had its origin" (*ED*: Preface). The only thing the author has invested in his books is an "almost fantastic hope." This too, is exactly as it should be.

Speaking of logic—and the preceding fugue was completely and perfectly logical, even if objectively empty—is it not the case that the question about the meaning of an authorship which begins in irony and indirection (which are impossible to put into non-opaque logical form), is by virtue of that fact a task which logic can only decide via a leap? That is to say, logic cannot decide. Logic cannot make decisions, though given certain definitions other things will certainly follow. Logic climbs from definitions, but a decision is a leap. As an ex-logician and philosopher, Johannes Climacus says in the context of his own interpretation of the pseudonymous works: "Whether my conception of the pseudonymous authors corresponds to what they themselves have had in mind, I cannot of course say, since I am only a reader; but it is clear enough that they bear a relationship to my thesis" (*CUPS*: 249).

I can be satisfied with that statement. And if my own *lille smule* is belittled because it is not objectively dogmatic ... well, be that as it may, it is always good to be distinguished by something, and I ask nothing better than to be pointed out as the only one who cannot make theses, and hence as the only one who does not understand what a piece of philosophy is. Very well; since I must have a point of view, let this stand:

The Point of View for my Work as an Author

It is possible that all this hullaballoo about the authorship, the pseudonyms, the replication of ironic content in ironic form in the writings of the poetically produced individualities is just that: hullaballoo. Maybe it is possible here to "deal with his writings as a critic usually does: Usually one deals with the writings and leaves the author out" (AR: 13). Kierkegaard himself suggests that this standard procedure is only out of place for one who has put himself forward as having had a revelation. For in the case of an apostle who writes Scripture one cannot "for one moment" forget the author. But for other authors, ... the question of who or what the author is is not of such decisive importance. All that is of importance is what one can learn from him. That learning may take several forms I do not doubt: one can learn facts about world history and semantics; one can also learn—from a different kind of author—that one is not what one has thought one was. This second kind of learning looks like a taking away of knowledge, but of course, it is not.

There is at least one problem with treating Kierkegaard as an ordinary author—one who is without authority; he himself presents it as a possibility: "purely imaginary and constructed with poetic license" (AR: 48). I will change it slightly to make my point clear. Suppose a highly reflective man—not a mere fisherman, as is usual in these cases—were to experience a revelation. Such a one would not—it must be pointed out—utilize reflection to test the revelation: is this really what it claims to be? Such an activity he would see immediately as a temptation. No. From the moment of the revelation his life is taken up by the higher power. He is completely aware of how communication can as well corrupt as edify, so the problem is to communicate the revelation in the correct form (*AR*: 75). If one had a revelation from God, the greatest danger would be that in communicating the revelation one's own self might be mistaken as the way to the truth, so that one's own self was what should be clung to rather than the revelation, and so that one's own self is one with whom it would be good to be seen at dinner. If one had a revelation from God, it would be perfectly clear to him that the really important thing is the revelation, from which point of view it would be indifferent whether or not one ever dined with the man himself.

So the first thing the man must do is to make himself repulsive. But this must be done in the appropriate fashion, in a way which keeps at the forefront the ever important demand that the revelation be communicated. The repulsion must therefore be one which makes no direct attack upon the established order, for such an attack either would draw attention away from the point of the revelation, or, in making oneself into a martyr, abuse the established order, which "is in intention just as tyrannous as when a tyrant mistreats men as slaves" (*AR*: 53).

Kierkegaard may have been this man. He was highly reflective. There was the mysterious Easter experience. He had an almost apostolic fear of gathering disciples to himself. He made himself repulsive—first to the Olsens, and then, during the Corsair affair, to all of Copenhagen—but never in a way which would draw a revolutionary, anti-establishment coterie around him. Unfortunately this theory fails: he had no revelation. Nothing that was a new starting point, only the old, "handed down from the fathers" Christianity.

Suppose, on the other hand he wanted to attack Christianity. Suppose he recognized in Christianity what Roland Barthes means by "myth"—a second order signification which transforms history into Nature, thus sucking the freedom from those under its spell. Barthes outlines what the mythologist must do:

> [He] cuts himself off from all the myth consumers, and this is no small matter. If this applied to a particular section of the collectivity, well and good. But when a myth reaches the entire community, it is from the latter that the mythologist must become estranged if he wants to liberate the myth. ... The mythologist is condemned to live in a theoretical sociality; for him, to be in society is, at best, to be truthful: his utmost sociality dwells in his utmost morality. His connection with the world is of the order of sarcasm.[17]

This theory could be what underlies Kierkegaard's praxis. As evidence I enlist the theoretical sociality of the pseudonyms, the sarcasm directed at Copenhagen, Denmark, philosophy, and everything held sacred in the entire community, including his refusal to worship in the Church of Denmark, to which he added the insult that it was for moral reasons.

Kierkegaard has already told a story similar to this one—that of Johannes Climacus' fateful relationship to the myth of philosophy in *De Omnibus Dubitandum Est*. What if Kierkegaard had attempted (as Johannes Climacus had with philosophy) to live out the

instructions of that old Christianity and found that it was
impossible? The teachers of Christianity were (as JC had found the
teachers of philosophy were) talking through their hats. He decided
to expose the illusion. He was reflective enough to know that a direct
attack from the outside would be of no avail. The only way to show
people they are in a cave is by turning their souls, chained by myth,
and somehow casting more light within the cave. So he became a
Christian author (or so he said). He maintained the lie
unshakably; illuminated from within the dark unreasonableness
of Christianity. He was defeated by it (as he knew he must be). He
exhibited from within that it is darkness and murderously
unreasonable to be—or even attempt to be—a Christian. Surely then
the world would get the message, and though he had to die for it, no
other earnest youth would be taken in to the great dark lie in which
he was buried. Somehow this nearly demonic (for the orthodox
interpreters of Kierkegaard) interpretation sounds closer to the truth
than the one which traces him back as one who was "in a line with
the apostles." The voice which whispers this idea makes it sound ...
temptingly credible.

Kierkegaard tells stories about writers—ones whom he
admires—who are capable of writing in such a way that the message
gets to the one who is to receive it while the heretics "get nothing to
run with." Assume the man is telling the truth. Assume that his
own writing is like that—for that one for whom it is intended not a
whisper, not a thought, not a kiss nor look is lost. For anyone else
the writing looks as plain as the sentences on this page. O do not ask
what religion the secret doctrine belongs to—the religion of the
seducer, or the true religion. (Though the gnostic tendency of this
description ought to make the orthodox uneasy.) Let us only ask

about the reader and the critic: How does the fair reader know she is the one addressed by the message which seems to be there? Could she then prove to the skeptics that it is indeed she who is "the one who, with humility and yet with a certain pride, I call my reader"? Or would the very act of proving that she is the beloved call into doubt that she was the receiver of the message—since it is not a message fit for all ears, and a proof *is* what is fit for all ears. What a questionable venture is it then to prove—perhaps before a committee, or for a coterie of journalistic reviewers—perhaps with style, wit and no little bit of irony—that one has understood the message and to bring that message and that proof before the public: Perhaps one's own ears are, in such a case, very long indeed.

This little essay is not meant to be a criticism of the community of ardent loving disciples gathering around Søren Kierkegaard. I myself would be a member of this community. But what reasonable human being believes that everything an ardent lover says about his beloved is true? Indeed, what ardent lover will believe another ardent lover except via the transference Shakespeare uses:

> So all their praises are but prophecies
> Of this our time, all you prefiguring(106),

which is precisely not to believe the other ardent lover. And even if two lovers should share the same beloved, would not both of them say—only seeming to agree—"so it is with my Regina."

What if I were to make a theory out of the poet's confessional practice here and say that to love is a certain way of reading, writing, marking and making signs so that all of them figure (or figure to) the beloved. Does Shakespeare in two lines, or 14, say all Barthes does in his lover's discourse? Here is my theory: Everyone wishes to be a philosopher. Nicolaus Notabene thinks so as well. Then this our time of post-structural post-modernism, which, in addition, often claims to be post-philosophical, is just another way of doing it (so to speak). For what does the "post" mean? Does "after" have significance for a sign among signs? How *can* it have significance? Doesn't it *have to* work this way: History is the movement of repression of the before. Post after post after post. Sign after sign. All our signs are but prophecies—and repressions.

Shakespeare's signs master both after and before—"this our time," (so always his time)—and us—we, who "have eyes to wonder, but lack tongues to praise." For his signs take no note of any change of time. Or tongue. We press the same signs into service—for our (whose?) use this time. We have eyes to see with, but lack tongues to praise—no new signs—so we press the old metal. This repression will not hold either; our face will fall away, rub off, our signing will no longer figure, or figure to. Under such conditions everything is always "post": *Sic semper thesesi.*

If we could but breathe and see, not sign, there would be no repression of one face for another, but without this repression we would be but brutes, unless we each were God and could create new praises out of nothing.[18]

II. An Algebraic Introduction to the Problem:
Either/Or

In knowledge there is no decision. But when a
man's knowledge has placed contrasting possibilities in equilibrium and he wants or has to judge,
then what he believes in becomes apparent, who he is.

——Søren Kierkegaard

Wer hat uns also umgedreht, daß wir
was wir auch tun, in jener Haltung sind
von einem welcher fortgeht?

——*Die Achte Elegie*, R. M. Rilke

Some questions do admit of an either/or. For example, this one:
"whether, besides philosophy, any further doctrine is required?"[19]
Leaving aside both what that "further doctrine" might be and also
what it might be required for—salvation, happiness, becoming a
professor, marrying well—let us examine the question for a
moment. Here are two ways to examine the question. Read either
the "A" examination or the "B" examination; both are set up
"algebraically."[20]

"A" Examination

Let us call the one who chooses the affirmative answer one who
affirms "X," where "X" is the unknown, since we are not sure what
it is such a one is affirming. If the answer to the question is
affirmative, then the following points, all of which are presented in
writings credited to SÅK, are perfectly sensible.

1. Philosophy is an essentially limited and incomplete enterprise.

2. That philosophy is not a completable enterprise is not discoverable by philosophy; it is, rather, revealed that there is something beyond the limits of human reason and human wisdom and it is also revealed that this something is required.

3. A teleological suspension of the ethical is possible.

Corollary of 2 and 3: A teleological suspension of the ethical has already occurred.

4. With respect to this "X" each person has to do directly with it and nothing to do directly with any other human being.

5. With respect to being an integral or authentic human being, the totality of objective relationships is insufficient either for description or achievement. This means that all human knowledge is both

    ◊ incomplete—"merely an approximation,"

    ◊ indecisive—not sufficient to move one to action.

6. Every human being is in a dreadful state until that which is outside reason's capacity makes its appearance in his life and he grasps for it (or it grasps him).

7. This "grasping for it" is not an extension of reason but a "leap" or "new birth."

    ◊ Thus, the appearance of this "X" provokes offense in reason.

    ◊ Furthermore, this "X" cannot afterward be accommodated to reason.

◊   No human being can help another to make this leap.

8. A human being cannot either begin to hope or rightly know what to hope for until the "X" = "something else necessary" provides both the condition and the capability.

Sed contra:

The true answer may be negative, in which case philosophy is a fully self-justifying *Wissenschaft* and Hamlet is mad to suggest that there are more things on heaven and earth or that philosophy is a dream. But one might well ask, if the answer is negative, what could have driven a thinker to ask the original question? What could so disturb that-than-which-nothing-more-is-required (i.e., human reason or philosophy) into asking "is there?"

If the answer is negative, then the following conclusions, all defended in the works of Kant, are completely reasonable.

1. Philosophy is essentially a completable enterprise.

2. That philosophy is a completable enterprise is a proposition within philosophy. (E.g. "The world is determined by the facts and by their being all the facts.")

3. Any suspension of the ethical is both moral evil and (if there is a God) sin.

4. If there is a God, he may be *primus*, but is clearly *inter pares* with regard to other rational beings. All such beings are directly related to each other *qua* rational beings.

5. The totality of objective relationships in the kingdom of ends would both allow and require authentic, integral human selfhood. That is to say:

◊ though our knowledge may now be incomplete, we can justifiably hope for our system of knowledge to be completed

◊ understanding may (Plato) or may not (Kant) be sufficient for motivating action, though in a completely rational being it would suffice.

6. A human being is only in a dreadful state when he acts irrationally.

7. If there is such a thing as religious faith it is eminently rational. That is:

◊ The religious is the completion or the core of reason.

◊ There is no question about the before or after of the appearance of the religious, it is co-eval with the appearance of reason.

◊ Everyone who is religious is religious in the same fully mediatable way.

8. Every rational being not only knows what to hope for, but also, insofar as he acts rationally, is actively hoping for it.

Respondeo:

Either the affirmative answer to the question is correct along with all that it entails, or the negative answer is correct, in which case the choice seems to be between Plato (who says that *knowledge is* virtue) and Kant (who says that *reason should be* sufficient for virtue). Because of claims like 7, the affirmative answer is often summarized as *"credo quia absurdum."* However, it should be obvious that these claims only allow *"credo atque absurdum est"*. This is directly opposing Kant, whose position with regard to moral faith is *"credo atque absurdum non est,"* that is, the moral world and its law are coherent with understanding and its laws. I am not sure that *credos* have *quias*. It would certainly be very strange to hold both that *credos* have *quias* and *credo quia absurdum*. A possible third way: "the [original Thomistic] question is one we are led to pose merely by the grammar of our language" promises that there is a way out of the fly-bottle. This "third way" is really a version of the negative answer, for philosophy—or an activity of reason—is what is going to show the fly the way out of the (merely linguistic or logical) fly-bottle. There is no third way.

"B" Examination

The Fifth Antinomy: One for Horatio

Thesis	*Antithesis*
There are more things on heaven and earth than are dreamt of in your philosophy.	There are not more things on heaven and earth than are dreamt of in my philosophy.
Implications	*Implications*
1. Philosophy is an essentially limited, incompletable enterprise.	1. Philosophy is an essentially completable enterprise.

2. That philosophy is not a completable enterprise is not discoverable by philosophy; it is, rather, revealed that there is something further than the limits of human reason and human wisdom and it is also revealed that this something is required.

3. A teleological suspension of the ethical is possible.

3.1 A teleological suspension of the ethical has already occurred.

4. With respect to this "further doctrine" each person has to do directly with it and nothing to do directly with any other human being.

5. With respect to being an integral, authentic, human being, the totality of objective relationships is insufficient for both description and achievement. This means that all human knowledge is both

5.1 incomplete—"merely an approximation,"

2. That philosophy is a completable enterprise is a proposition within philosophy. E.g., "The world is determined by the facts and by their being *all* the facts."

3. Any suspension of the ethical is both moral evil and (if there is a God) sin.

4. If there is a God, he may be *primus*, but he is clearly *inter pares* with regard to other rational beings. All such beings are directly related to each other *qua* rational beings.

5. The totality of objective relationships in the kingdom of ends would both allow and require authentic, integral selfhood. That is to say,

5.1 though our knowledge may now be incomplete, we can justifiably hope for our system of knowledge to be completed and

5.2 indecisive—not sufficient to move one to action.

5.2 understanding may (Plato), or may not (Kant), be sufficient for motivating action, though in a purely rational being it would suffice.

6. Every human being is in a dreadful state until that which is outside reason's capacity makes its appearance in his life and he grasps for it (or it him).

6. A human being is only in a dreadful state when he acts irrationally.

7. This "grasping for it" is not an extension of reason but a "leap" or "new birth."

7. If there is such a thing as religious faith, it is eminently rational. That is,

7.1 Thus, the appearance of this "X" (the further doctrine) provokes offense in reason.

7.1 The religious is the completion or the core of reason. (There is no further doctrine.)

7.2 Furthermore, this "X" cannot afterward be accommodated to reason.

7.2 There is no question about the before or after of the appearance of the religious; it is co-eval with the appearance of reason.

7.3 No human being can make this leap for, or help another make, this leap.

7.3 Every religious person is religious in the same, fully mediatable way.

8. A human being can not either begin to hope or rightly know what to hope for until the "X" = "something else necessary" provides both the condition and the capability.

8. Every finite rational being not only knows what to hope for, but also, insofar as he acts rationally, is actively hoping for it.

Observations on the Fifth Antinomy

On the Thesis	*On the Antithesis*

These claims are all presented in writings credited to Kierkegaard. Because of such claims his position has been summarized as *"credo quia absurdum."* It should, however, be obvious that these claims (especially 7 and 8) only allow *"credo atque absurdum est."* I am not sure that *credos* have *quias*. It would certainly be very strange to hold both that *"credos* have *quias* and *"credo quia absurdum."*

These claims are all defended by Kant and are completely reasonable. In fact one could summarize this position as at least *"credo atque absurdum non est,"* that is the moral world and its law are coherent with understanding and its laws. But it would probably be more precise to say this position is *credo quia intelligo* since if you know what knowledge, including knowledge of the moral imperative, requires, you will have "moral faith." Some philosophers choose this path thinking that they have found a third way: we are led to pose the question by the grammar of our language. That path is the same as this one, for it will be an activity of reason which gets us out of the bottle of our language.

Both "A" and "B" Examinations

Of course, it may be that the person holding the affirmative answer to the question is leading one away from the truth. In which case he is a seducer *par excellence*, for by laying out the implications of the affirmative answer we can see that there is no check upon this path—no re/cognizable check. In fact, it sounds as if the first step on that path is: turn your back not only on what you have thought to be the truth, but also on what you thought to be the way to the truth. It may also be that the negative answer is false, but if it is, it would be very difficult to say how we *know* that it is so. One can *either* answer Aquinas' first question affirmatively and allow oneself to be led (astray?), *or* answer the question by denial, thereby refusing to be led (to the truth?). These are all merely dialectical necessities following upon asking a question; they imply nothing actual in any possible world. Kant and Kierkegaard may both have ontological commitments due to their answers to these questions; I, however, have none since I am deciding nothing, but merely asking a question. As yet I have no thesis.

Anti-Climacus poses another such *either/or* question, indirectly, to his reader. He defines a self as "a relation which relates itself to its own self" and continues, "such a relation ... must either have constituted itself or have been constituted by another" (*SUD*: 146). What this other Power is he does not immediately say, so let us call it X also. Now the problem is set up as it should be, so that the question about philosophy is at the same time a question about oneself: Whether or not besides reason anything else is necessary?

There is a parting of the ways here. While I am especially interested in the eighth conclusion entailed by each answer, it is important to see that each answer is decisive about a whole range of philosophical issues, as well as the "existential" problem of how either "I am" or, more philosophically, "one" is to live life. We can look down both paths, at least for a while, but we cannot travel both and remain one traveller. That Kant and Kierkegaard seem to diverge so clearly at this point is a little surprising if one considers that they agree on what faith is. At least, they agree when the

formula is given algebraically. Anti-Climacus defines faith as
"that the self in being itself and in willing to be itself is grounded
transparently in God" (*SUD*: 213). Kant's moral argument for the
existence of God, which is the proof of practical faith, depends on just
this point of getting clear about what it is to will as a moral self: it is
to will the complete good, which is only achievable through the
concomitant working of the moral ruler of the universe. Thus
reason's categorical imperative is grounded in God (for whom the
imperative is simply the law of being). Hence the clear-thinking
moral agent "in willing to be itself is [also] grounded transparently
in God." One step beyond this agreement—or maybe it is the step
before: how does this grounding occur?—and the two are on different
paths, as outlined in the foregoing examinations.

The Question of Hope

According to our algebraic introduction the matter stands thus: If
one affirms X—thus the first side of the dilemma—it is idolatry to
hope for anything other than what (or for any other reason than that)
the Unknown reveals it. If one disbelieves X, then hope rides on the
coattails of knowledge. Hope rides on just such coattails for Kant.
But by extending practical reason where theoretical reason can not
go, he pushes hope quite far out on this road. Hegel, Kierkegaard's
favorite target, brings hope so far in that it becomes a sublated
moment in absolute knowing—there is (really) room for neither
hope nor despair. Kierkegaard pushes the whole problem down
another road entirely.

Though Kant pushes hope out of the realm of understanding and
into that of practical faith, it is still the case for him that hope is

grounded in human knowledge: We know we are under a categorical imperative to achieve the complete good. If it were known to be impossible to achieve that good, it would be giddy romanticism or the absentmindedness of despair to hope for it. But, Kant argues, the project of morality cannot be shown to be impossible; therefore, hope for a kingdom where happiness accords with deserts is, as an internal requirement of morality, perfectly reasonable.

But the ethical project outlined by Kant is impossible. And it is impossible for reasons which are intrinsic to that project. First, it is impossible for the finite rational will to rigorously fulfill the moral law. To be given eternity to do so does not resolve the question. Kant realized this and, in the *Religion*, added to the idea of a will approaching perfection in a continuing life, a doctrine of atonement for failure, in order to overcome the problem of the inability of the will. But this answer only multiplies impossibilities:

1. A will can only be approaching (or falling from) perfection as temporal, but the will is, for Kant, not a temporal phenomenon.

2. Atonement by another moral being would result in three further problems:

◊ increase the guilt of the already imperfect will—since its imperfections required the sacrifice.

◊ change the moral personality (which is the personality) from without. Whether or not this is heteronomous it is at least not by the will's own working, but by the power of another, in which case the moral personality is not one's own.

◊ destroy the agreement of happiness and desert in the kingdom of ends. For if both more and less perfect wills are

granted the grace of atonement their imperfections would be
equally well atoned for and so the moral personalities would
be equally and undeservedly happy.

There is nothing else to be done but to let this hope grounded in
the moral law die. That does not mean one must become a believer
of X. There are at least two ways of dying: suicide is one. Moral
suicide would be to kill the moral impulse in oneself as a seducing
siren's song—or call it a ghost story. Any number of other means
are available—call them forms of euthanasia: the hemlock of
cynicism, an overdose of romanticism, the steel razor of fascism.
These are not radical cures, but only escapes. Perhaps only
attempted escapes. The radical cure is, as Anti-Climacus says,
"simply to die, to 'die from'" (SUD: 143).

How is it that "dying from" is a cure, while suicide and
euthanasia are not? Here is what Anti-Climacus means by "die
from:" Since the self is a relation which relates itself to itself by
grounding itself in the power which constituted it, and this power
may be either oneself or some X, the radical cure is to die from
grounding one's hopes in a project constituted by oneself. It would
also seem to imply dying from grounding one's hopes in a project
constituted by another self, since, insofar as that self is like oneself,
it is equally inadequate. It is also clear that very few of the other
powers surrounding one could make any claim to being the power
which constituted one's own self—making them even less adequate
than one's self as the ground for one's hope.

* * *

In the first chapter I will argue that the problem of hope is central to certain kinds of philosophical project like Kant's and Kierkegaard's: in general any project which involves an essential task. In particular, the second part of that chapter will show how the problem of hope arises in Kant's speculative philosophy but that an answer cannot be grounded there. The second chapter gives Kant's practical defense of hope and then shows how the contradictions mentioned above make that defense hopeless.

The third chapter will examine the virtue of hope as it appears in several characters in Kierkegaard's drama. The virtue turns out to be either dishonest or a blatant absurdity. This sounds not only radical, but dangerous; perhaps nihilistic, perhaps leading to fascism: one should die *from* morality? Yes, but what matters is how: die from the moral project grounded in reason, but not from being a self, which the cynic, romantic and fascist all aim to do. There is a change at the root: The most important question, put in the place of Kant's "what must I do?" is "what can God do?" Everything. "God is that all things are possible."[21] What follows from this? Moral quietism? Possibly, but certainly not necessarily; and nothing in the work of SÅK indicates anything like it. (How could work be an indication of quietism anyway?) In fact, Kierkegaard takes the opposite stance. Faith, transparently grounding oneself in the Power (which is that all things are possible) which constituted the self, and which Power thereby is the ground of one's hope, requires love, which means "to have come into infinite debt" (*WL*: 181). And so faith implies duty, the converse of Kant's view that duty implies faith. Or perhaps these theses are not opposed.

Chapter 1:

THE CENTRALITY OF HOPE

I: Task/Self/Hope

Warum, wenn es angeht also die Frist des Daseins
hinzubringen, als Lorbeer, ein wenig dunkler als alles
andere Grün, mit kleinen Wellen an jedem
Blattrand (wie eines Windes Lächeln)—: warum dann
Menschliches müssen—und, Schicksal vermeidend,
sich sehnen nach Schicksal?

—*Die Neunte Elegie*, R. M. Rilke

Human beings can take on many tasks. Perhaps no other animal is as adaptable to or as creative of new tasks. Why not? Were I misanthropic I would say no other animal has so much to escape from. If either Kant or Kierkegaard had been given to a hermeneutic of suspicion, perhaps they would have said so. Certainly they both agree that human beings have tasks which, unlike our more ordinary ones, are essential to the kind of being we are. Tasks which are, as it were, assigned—by Nature or by nature's God—or assigned by Reason. It is, of course, also possible that such tasks are self-assigned, or perhaps we merely think we have a task and think of it as assigned by something greater than our sole self in order to make our doing of the task count for more than mere self-aggrandizement or self-entertainment.

However that may be, Kant and Kierkegaard agree that there are tasks which are essential to every human being. They disagree

about what the task is, how we know it, what makes the task possible
and what makes it essential. That, for the moment, we can put aside
in order to focus on this area of agreement: What is an essential
task? What are the conditions for the possibility of being a sort of
thing with an essential task?

In order for a task[1] to belong essentially to a being, the being
must have the same essential structure as a task: the being must be
one that is becoming. An ordinary task is always becoming.
Before it is assigned there is no task. If something is a perfected
work, then it is no longer a task. Between assignment and perfected
work is the task, which is a becoming since it lies between non-
existence and perfection. If the task is avoided and not begun then it
is a possible task—but an essential task would be an evolving
actuality, not a possibility, whenever the being which has it exists.
To speak Greek: a task is a *kinesis*, not an *ousia*, or perhaps better,
its *ousia* is *kinesis* Such a task is, then, always already begun if the
being exists. It may be possible that an essential task can be ignored
or left unworked upon, but unlike a more mundane task, like
writing (or reading) a book, an essential task could never be
abandoned. Nor would ignoring such a task change the fact that it
is the task (unlike changing one's mind about writing the book),
and so it does not change the fact that the task is becoming even
when there is no movement towards the goal. On the other hand, if
an essential task were to be perfected, the being which has it as an
essential task would become a different kind of being. A task is an
essentially temporal kind of thing, like existing human beings.

A task is a thing which has its own *telos* within it. It has its own
definition of what is to count as completion. The person who is

assigned a task cannot say, e.g., "I will work on this for a couple hours and then be done with it." And the person who has assigned a task cannot interrupt one's work and say "consider it finished" when it is not finished, except by changing the task. For an essential task this means that finishing the task and an essential change in the being will be concomitant. If there is an essential task for a human being, then to finish that task will be to become something other than human. When a task is assigned the dialectic is to do or not to do. When a task is essential that dialectic collapses into the dialectic of Hamlet.

It is possible that there are impossible tasks. Mythology is full of stories about assigning impossible tasks to half-divine heroes and heroines. It is even possible that there are impossible tasks which are essential. A being which had one would be a useless passion. And would engage in useless action. And both essentially; it would be incapable, on its own power, of doing what it was supposed to do. Yet it would be driven to attempt it, or to atone for not completing it.[2] A being which has a task essentially will also have certain characteristic actions and passions essentially, since any task implies both. A task, like any becoming, implies a relation between what is and what is not. A being which has a task essentially will be a being which relates this relation of being to non-being. It will be that relation. Such a relation to the second power Kierkegaard, or specifically Anti-Climacus, calls a self.[3]

In the ordinary sense, if one has a task—like writing a book defending a particular philosophical thesis—it can be avoided. In many ways. But neither a book nor the making or defense of philosophical theses are essential tasks. An essential task, if there is such a thing, is the kind of thing that if you are avoiding it, then you are attempting to avoid yourself. Here a psychologist may step in and give any number of theories explaining why this might occur or how it might be attempted, but the philosophical point is the one about the condition for the possibility of any such psychological hermeneutic and that condition is that the self *is* this task, and an essential task is a relation (of necessity to possibility, among other things). And since the task is a relation we can say that the self is a relation which relates itself to itself.[4] Since the relation to the task is essential, avoidance is impossible and all avoidance is work on the task, albeit in the direction of undoing it. Having an essential task implies that all of one's action is on the task; one can only change direction, not escape it altogether. If there is no essential task then there is no direction home and

> we are here as on a darkling plain
> Swept with confused alarms of struggle and flight
> Where ignorant armies clash by night.[5]

With regard to these two choices there is no middle ground. It is either/or: *Either* an essential task and then either doing it or undoing it, *Or* no essential task and then whatever is possible has no essential meaning. That seems trivially true, but in fact meaningfulness seems altogether impossible since without any essential meaning there is no reasonable way to conceive of conferring meaning. One cannot confer a power one does not have, one can only pretend to do so, or be misled into thinking one has the power to do so. (As Malvolio is misled into thinking he has the power to correct his mistress' kinsmen in *Twelfth Night*.) If free choice is to confer even temporary or local meaning on human action, freedom itself must be seen as essentially meaningful and freedom as an essential task of a human being. Sartre seems to follow this line of thought. But it should be noted that such a move is just one type of the philosophy which defines man as having an essential task and though what it means to say that freedom is a task may be extremely difficult to explicate, such a philosophy is not an example of the second path—there is no essential task.

It should be obvious that any philosopher who has an essential task involved in his idea of human nature will have an ethic built in—more or less consciously—to his theory. We might, in other words, change Karamazov's claim to "if there is no essential task, then everything is permitted." What such an editorial change would lose in musicality and wit, it more than makes up for in pedantry. The general consensus seems to be that the more consciously the ethic is built in to the theory the less suspect the theory is, since its agenda is not hidden. His straightforwardness in this regard is one of Kant's excellences. A deeper excellence is that the doctrine of the primacy of practical reason together with his argument for the moral unity of the world (both of which will be taken up in detail below) intimates that what we are always about in the world is our moral vocation—in one way or another we are about it even now. The Good may not always be at stake, but each person's good is. The unity of the world is a moral unity—*or not*. It should be clear then, that I do not agree with those contemporary interpreters of Kant who say things like "Kant wants the lines drawn ... to be sharp, ... margins clean, the right hand of science clearly set off from the left hand of values."[6]

Having an essential task implies having passions. Since a task has an implicit *telos*, having a task essentially means being moved by, being affected by, either desiring or hating the implied *telos* of the task. A task in the ordinary sense arouses one from lethargy, and if a task is essential, being affected is unavoidable. And why would one move to avoid something anyway? Isn't such a movement an indication of passion—the movement of the appetitive power in relation to an object? And if the "object" is an essential task—then the movement of the appetitive power in relation to its proper object. But one of these two phrases is just what the definition of a passion is.[7]

If there is an essential task for a self, then the self will have one of two passions depending on whether the *telos* of the essential task is considered possible or not. The human being, if it has an essential task, lives either in hope or in despair. If the task is essential, there can be no middle ground: it is either/or. Here the issue seems to turn on one of knowledge: what is considered possible? It is at this point that Kant and Kierkegaard begin to separate, for up to this point they would both have agreed with this exposition.[8]

Now it begins to be clear why Kant says that "the third question [about hope] is at once practical and theoretical" (A805/B8343 and that answering it provides "the sole means of reconciling the speculative with the practical interest" (A742/B770). Reason has two essential tasks—one speculative, one practical. These tasks are prescribed by reason to itself, it is true, but according to Kant's conception of Reason[9] it can do no other. The tasks are at once self-assigned and essential. A plethora of problems ensues from this conjunction. Kant thinks they are resolvable. Perhaps they are not, but what is important here is the necessity of the connection between the "essential interests of reason" and the passional dialectic of hope/despair.

Kant clearly is in agreement with this explication of essential tasks, for in his definition of interest he hits upon both the point that such a thing is subject to the dialectic of "to be or not to be" and that it is necessarily tied to the passions:

> To will something and to take delight in its existence, i.e. to take an interest in it, are identical (*KU*: 209).

> The delight which we connect with the representation of the real existence of an object is called interest. Such a delight, therefore, always involves a reference to the faculty of desire, either as its determining ground, or else as necessarily implicated with its determining ground (*KU*: 204).

Willing and interest are intrinsically connected with to be, not not to be. Reason has two tasks essentially. As essential tasks Reason necessarily is interested in the real existence of the *telos* of each task. Since the tasks are essential, their *teloi* are either coming into existence or ceasing to be.

The two tasks Reason presents are the bases of Kant's twofold division of philosophy into the laws of nature and the laws of freedom. The interests of Reason are to know the one and to act in accord with the other. Reason's *teloi* are a complete *Naturwissenschaft* and the complete good. The articles "a" and "the" are not at all accidental in Kant's view. Since our knowledge of nature is effected through sensuous intuition and such forms, while universally human, are not necessarily the only ones possible, our science of nature—even when complete—will only be one and though we cannot know in any other way it is anthropomorphic hubris to call our *Wissenschaft* "the" science of nature. It is, on the other hand, not only impractical, but impossible to seek knowledge of or through any other forms of intuition.   A *Wissenschaft* is knowledge; what we can know of things is limited, but the way things can be in themselves may not be so strictly limited.

Ethics, on the contrary, is based solely on pure reason, which even in us limited creatures can in and of itself be practical—be the source of maxims. Therefore there is one ethic, one complete good at which our, and every rational being's, moral maxims aim.

The first question to which Reason requires an answer then, is "can we hope for a complete *Naturwissenschaft*, and if so, on what basis?" The second question is: "can we hope for the complete good, and if so, on what basis?" They are Hamletian questions—what can I know (of this ghost)? What must I do?—but these questions are not posed by anything external—the rotten state of Denmark, say— rather they are dictated by Kant's understanding of the essential tasks of Reason and the essential tasks of Rational beings generally. The remainder of this chapter will pursue the first complex question. The second chapter will pursue the second.

II: Hope in Kant's Speculative Philosophy, or;
De Reductione Scientiae ad Bonos Mores

> To think is first of all to create a world (or to limit
> one's own world, which comes to the same thing).
> The philosopher, even if he is a Kant, is a creator. He
> has his characters, his symbols, and his secret
> action. He has his plot endings.
>   ——Albert Camus

How the Question of Hope Arises

The first edition of Kant's *Critique of Pure Reason* opens on a tone of
hopelessness expressed in poetry from Sophocles to Matthew
Arnold's "Dover Beach." Like the later poem, the first *Critique*
affords its despair by investing all its funds in the one remaining
possibility. That one remaining possibility seems a small and
circumscribed vessel in comparison with the vast seas surrounding
both speakers, but both Arnold and Kant hope to show that she is safe
and sea-worthy. Both writers—who figure the vessel of their hope as
a woman—vow to be true to their task and carry it out so far as their
power makes them capable. Kant is aware, as both the first *Critique*
and "Preface" to the *Prolegomena* show, that others have placed
their hopes in just this same so-called queen, yet those hopes have
never been fulfilled. He is sure that his work will persuade her to
turn over a new leaf—to be reborn. He hopes that he will succeed
where his predecessors have failed because what he proposes is a
rebirth that is in her own interest and in accord with her own
natural principles—it is not the induced labor of dogmatism or the
sterile abortion of skepticism.

As a philosopher Kant awakens from his dogmatic slumbers

(with the same woman) to find himself and his queen in just that very nearly hopeless dramatic situation that is given voice in his book and in Arnold's poem. That both he and *Metaphysica*, his queen, are in such dire straits is partially his own fault, since he himself had been sailing uncritically by the flawed charts of the dogmatists (slumbering dogmatically in the soiled sheets—the unnatural mixture of metaphors is Kant's). There is a history of such mistakes behind him—the history of philosophy—a history which makes his own error more understandable perhaps, perhaps makes his error more difficult to avoid, but a history which does not absolve him, or make his original ... error less his or less an error. The dramatic project of Kant's authorship is for the newly awakened hero to redeem the reputation of his queen (a task perhaps just as difficult—just as morally questionable?—as Lancelot's defense of Guinevere from the charge of adultery) and lead her and her faithful band of citizen-sailors to a land of freedom and light, safe harbor, shelter and home.

That, at least is how the rhetoric moves at the beginning. By the end of the first *Critique*, however, it sounds more like the queen is a woman we should neither marry nor attempt to make fruitful, though she is a continual enticement.[10] The Kantian project is, under either rhetoric, one with essentially moral aims, and it is so even when it is stated in terms of knowledge: "Criticism alone can sever the root of materialism, fatalism, atheism, free-thinking, fanaticism and superstition, which can be injurious universally, as well as of idealism and skepticism" (B xxxiv).

If we had to choose between Kant's early dogmatism and the other choice extant before his awakening—empiricism—we would, Kant thinks, prefer dogmatism because it renders possible the

completion of the edifice of knowledge (A474/B502). The
architectonic interest of reason makes a complete *Naturwissenschaft* an essential task for human beings. Empiricism is not
merely a recurring deferral of this speculative interest of Reason, it
is a denial of its very possibility. Quite naturally, it ends in
Hume's skepticism. Reason can make do with a deferral of its
interests, but since interest is connected to real existence, denial of
the possibility of the real existence of a complete *Naturwissenschaft*
would be the despair, if not the death, of Reason. If empiricism were
the whole truth about knowledge, science would be a useless passion.
This is not to say that science would not be effective. Tang® and
mini-computers would still be invented, but the passion which
drives the scientific enterprise is not a passion for Tang® or mini-
computers, it is the architectonic interest of Reason and that passion,
according to the dogmas of empiricism, is empty. A consistent
empiricism would transfer the hopes of the scientific enterprise to
technical proficiency. And it would allow that science could be
driven by any number of other human motivations. Science itself
could then claim to be a sort of value-free enterprise—a suitable
attachment to any *telos* proposed by any group or individual. The
hope within the task of science would then be only the hope for
achievement of the *telos* to which the enterprise is attached. If one
were to choose the side of empiricism these consequences would
follow necessarily. But as it is, it is not. There is no such division
between the world of facts and the world of values. Kant's whole
argument is aiming to show that the as yet untrodden critical path
allows empiricism its effectiveness without making Reason, in
particular its theoretical scientific enterprise, a useless passion, or
worse, a useful whore.

The other pre-critical choice—dogmatism—while seeming to
fulfill Reason's architectonic interest is, in reality, mere fabri-
cation, not knowledge. By dogmatism some might misunderstand
Kant to be criticizing the philosophy of the whole preceding
millennium. But any great medieval philosopher would ask the
same kind of questions, and need to make the same kind of
distinctions, as Kant does. Scotus, for example, would ask
"Whether there are any necessary truths about contingent things?"
Furthermore, he would answer, as Kant does, that there are
necessary truths about both contingent things and a free will.
Kant's *Critiques* investigate the sources of our knowledge in order
to make similar distinctions. The philosophy developed in the
Critiques makes it possible not only to distinguish between kinds of
knowledge and truth—empirical and *a posteriori* versus necessary
and *a priori*—but also to separate knowledge from poetry and
science from art.[11] On all of these distinctions neither the
dogmatists nor the empiricists could ever hold the line. Kant leaves
it to the third *Critique* to finally tie down all, but most directly, the
last of those distinctions. Consequently, if the third *Critique* fails in
its intrinsic purpose it is not Kant's aesthetics which is called into
question, still less his ethics, but fundamentally, whether scientific
knowledge is distinctively different from poetry, or a good life from
a work of art. Where radical empiricism reduces everything to the
happy (or less happy) accidentality of poetry, dogmatism makes all
the world an *a priori* crystalline structure formed in the pure
gravityless mind of God.

Enough lyric. We commonly recognize a distinction between
true and false, good and evil. Kant begins by taking a step back and

asking what makes these distinctions—true/false, good/evil—possible? His answer is that whereas other creatures submissively follow the law of nature, man has an impulse leading him to set up some other law to control the bent of his nature. Were this fact false, the two distinctions would not be possible: There could be no such thing as truth, for truth and falsity depend upon the distinction between ideality (the general form of that "other law" set up by man) and nature.[12] Ideality is used to control nature, to control the behavior of the experimenter in the empirical investigation of nature, to set up a route and pattern for understanding the whole of nature, including the ideally controlled experimenter within it. The experiment is to investigate whether nature acts in accord with the ideal or not. Without this distinction between ideality and nature the distinction between truth and falsity evaporates into brute facticity. The facticity that what is, is, and brutish because there is no thought about what is. In addition to this first point, there could be no such thing as right or duty providing a counterweight to pleasure, cleverness, wealth or happiness as motives for human acting. But, says Kant, the common understanding sees a distinction between these motives and refuses to recognize any of them as a moral one. The common recognition that there is such a distinction would not be possible if impulses of nature were all human beings acted on and were it not the case that human beings do set up some other law for their actions over against all of those natural impulses. A principle not *of* nature, but *in* it, which claims to sit in judgement over all of those natural impulses.

The condition for the possibility of both of these types of other laws, which are the creation of reason in its speculative and practical workings, is, at its root, the same thing: It must be the case that what we will to achieve ever exceeds the boundaries of our knowledge. Were things otherwise science would be transubstantiated from discursive propositions about things to creative intuition of them. That is the only way to have one's will coextensive with one's knowledge. Or, on the other hand, morality's "ought" would become a holy "is" were one's knowledge to extend farther than one's will. Perhaps this latter extreme could be called angelic, as opposed to brutish, facticity.[13]

Science and morality are attempts to become like God. Unless we are really to become God it must be granted that we cannot reach the point at which knowledge is either co-extensive with or extends farther than our willing. That neither of these two points can ever be reached, not merely in fact, but in principle, is Kant's view of the human predicament.[14] We are beings for whom all the knowledge that is possible for us cannot extend so far as our willing. For things to be otherwise is no longer to be human. Call the range of possible knowledge phenomenal, and what is not within our range noumenal. The purpose of those words is to mark out the predicament of man, not to give metaphysicians or ontologists a place to start. Any being whose intellect and will are coextensive, or whose intellect extends farther than his will has no such distinction. Brutes don't have it. God doesn't have it. Human beings do. But if this is our predicament so long as we are human, how can we human beings have any hope?

Defer that troublesome question for a moment. If this distinction is clear, then it should also be clear that to ask Kant a question like "does this noumenal world have many things in it or one?" is exactly like asking his more mundane neighbor "have you stopped beating your wife yet?" For in both cases either answer vitiates the claim which is really at issue: In Kant's case the claim is that there are things we cannot, in principle, know; in his neighbor's case the claim is that he is and always has been a good and kindly husband.

The duality of the human predicament is the basic fact Kant's project begins from. When he asks "what can I know? what must I do?" he is not directing the question to the nature of intelligence or willing in general, still less is he asking it from the standpoint of a hypostatized Absolute Spirit. He wants to know what a sensible (thus finite), finite (therefore discursive) Reason can possibly know and what a human (thus finite), rational (therefore free) will must do. It is just this predicament, on Kant's view, that makes critique the task of the philosophical faculty and it is the permanence of the predicament that makes critique the permanent task of the philosopher (*SdF*: 55 and, obliquely, 45).

These points strike me as basic to Kant's view throughout his critical period;[15] in addition, they seem to be correct about the human way of being. Thus far it seems that the problem of knowledge and the demand of morality are at least parallel problems. Understanding aims at an end (a unified world) which cannot be an object for it (since we cannot have an intuition of the world). Morality aims at an end which it does not achieve (in what we experience of the world happiness does not accord with desert). In both projects our achievement is limited; both aim at "essential interests of reason;" both are essential tasks for rational creatures. Kant, however, also sees them as as inseparable and unintelligible apart from each other as printed foreground and white background on this page. His reasoning, the details of which will be seen clearly by the end of this chapter, is that scientific knowledge is intrinsically tied up with an idea whose proper place is the practical philosophy. That idea is the unity of the world. Now, if knowledge and morality are unintelligible apart from one another, it seems that labelling one foreground and the other background is an arbitrary choice, just as you might read this print as background breaking through the pale foreground. One common way of reading Kant—with the practical philosophy in the background and epistemology foremost—does just this. But though his pages are intelligible this way, it is not the way Kant himself reads those pages. Since "all the interests of my reason" are united in three questions, and those three questions are united in the question about hope, and that question is deferred to the practical philosophy, it is evident that Kant himself takes epistemological questions as background. Perhaps even his way of asking the question "what are the grounds for the possibility of knowledge?" guarantees that epistemological considerations will be background.

Kant's resolution of what had been accepted as the problem of knowledge after Descartes takes a turn into the problem of the grounds for the possibility of communication because of his redefinition of objectivity in terms of intersubjectivity. Kant sees, in other words, that the two defining problems of epistemology— certainty and communication—must be resolved at once. The simpler treatment of them as separate problems exhibits the fact that if one of them is resolved without reference to the other, the second will never be resolved. We can see this inverse relationship of certain solution and irresolvable problem clearly in the history of philosophy. Descartes can be treated as one asymptote of the hyperbola, for he resolves the problem of certainty completely, but in so doing he buries himself in the other. Absolute skepticism is absolutely defeated by his famous (but poverty-stricken, by Augustinian standards) argument, but the problems of other minds: how do we know them, how do we know of them, how do we communicate with them—or can we know, know of, communicate with them are his irresolvable legacy to rationalistic philosophy. A philosophy which ends, quite appropriately, in windowless monads. It seems that certainty is in some important respects a psychological thing—a mental state or event—and so long as mental events are thought of purely as one's own, certainty, as one such mental state, will also be just that—purely one's own: incommunicable.

A pure and simple pragmatism seems to be the other asymptotic endpoint of the epistemological problem. A pragmatist works with other minds all the time. The epistemological problem of certainty does not come up for the pragmatist, familiar as he is with the fact that all his science is an exercise in statistical modeling. But the pragmatist can't answer Descartes' evil genius question: what if this is all a mass hallucination? "What do you mean," he responds, "it works, doesn't it?" Philosophically this answer is (at least in the tradition) a cut below the appeal to Divinity, because whereas Descartes admits that there is a problem of certainty in knowledge and calls on God to guarantee the truth of clear and distinct ideas, the pragmatist throws the whole problem out because its solution has no practical consequences. Since the solution (if there were one) to the epistemological problem has no practical consequences, the solution is not regarded as knowledge by the healthy pragmatist. But clearly, if all our experience were an inescapable spell cast by an evil genius, knowing that would be a piece of knowledge, useless though it be. *Perhaps* Descartes' appeal to Divinity and the pragmatist's appeal to getting things done are the only answers possible, but a philosopher will put himself out of work if he admits that so easily.

Pragmatism works pretty well when a group of people are talking about achieving a certain goal and already have a tacit agreement on either the kind of end the community is trying to achieve or the ways in which ends (including coming to agreement on ends) can be achieved. But what if there are two communities which have no such tacit agreement on either score, as for example, the Bikini Islanders and the U.S. government? Certainly we have our ways of getting things done in these cases too. But does one call that communication? One way to understand Kant's project in relation to the pragmatist's is by seeing that he is attempting to explore the grounds of that tacit agreement which allows pragmatists to talk with each other.

To tie this discussion back to the erotic metaphors with which we began, we can wonder what kind of relationship Mr. Arnold imagines with his new wife, and similarly, what Sir Immanuel's intentions are with regard to his soon to be rehabilitated queen. As John V. Smyth illustrates in a similar discussion of Hegel, Socrates and Kierkegaard,[16] the philosophical knight might end up grasping, holding and making fruitful—which is what love really means if you ask any empiricist or pragmatist (Alcibiadeses all)— or the knight may only wish to assist the queen to her complete manifestation so that he may contemplate her more perfectly, all the while allowing her to remain inviolate—as a rationalist, platonist or mystic would: to look, divest, and see, but not to conquer, no, not even touch. In both cases, it will be noted, only the erotic intentions of the male are asked about: it may be that Sir Immanuel misperceives his queen, or that Mr. Arnold misreads his dear wife's silence.[17]

What if truth *is* a woman? What is the underside of all these erotic economies? Does it make a difference what the philosopher's intentions are in doing philosophy? Might there not be certain intentions in making theses (and I suppose other intentions in asking questions)? Is the difference in erotic economy a difference between honorable and dishonorable intentions? Is the difference in erotic economy merely a difference in taste (about which there can be no dispute), or is it aesthetic (about which there may be contention)? Or might it not be an ethically, or even religiously, motivated difference, like a refusal to marry might be?

Kant's clear uniting of the problems of certainty and communication is correct. His attempted answer is, if inadequate, not due to seeing the problem wrongly. The search he engaged in was for a non-solipsistic grounding of knowledge, or, in other words, a communicable transcendentalism. The first way of stating the issue "non-solipsistic grounding of knowledge" is indicative of the fact that Kant's critique of rationalism goes right to the heart of the *Meditations*. The second way of stating the issue—"communicable transcendentalism"—brings out the fissure in Kant's own works, for communication is certainly phenomenal and transcendentalism certainly is not. That there are nearly as many interpretations of Kant as there are Kant scholars indicates that there is a major hermeneutical problem with his work. Stating the project in the second way puts that problem in the forefront. In more typically Kantian terms we could ask "what are the grounds for the possibility of communication?" (Note that if this question says anything to you, it also makes it look like there should be an answer.) Kant's own way of asking the question—what are the grounds for the possibility of any knowledge whatsoever—leans closer to the skeptical side of the epistemological hyperbola. I suppose he words things that way in order to cut more clearly at the root of rationalism, which was the reigning philosophy in the German universities of his day. The question which aims at pragmatism is just as legitimate, just as *critical*.

Whatever Kant's motivating intention, it is clear that he saw this hyperbola as a major part of the framework of the critical project, for he saw that "conviction" and its look alike but dishonest brother, "persuasion," could not be distinguished by the person who claims to know a certain fact just by looking at the claim each brother puts forth: X is Y.[18] For example, Winston, in *1984* writes in his diary that 2+2=4. Later he says 2+2=5. He cannot tell by mere inspection of the claims which one he is persuaded of and which he is convinced of. Kant explains that the critical test in every case is the possibility of communicating it and finding it valid for all reasoning beings. The problem of Descartes method is recognized here, for his *Cogito* can neither be binding upon anyone else nor bind him to anyone else—that is, no one else can be convinced of Descartes' existence by it nor can he himself be convinced of anyone else's existence (barring revelation of course, which, I suppose, supplies its own Truth Maker). If Descartes had sought conviction rather than certainty he would have had no problem with solipsism.

When one is *persuaded*, the ground of judgement is solely in the subject, but is regarded as objective. This is Winston's case when he says that 2+2=5. He really does regard it as objective. The lie is given to persuasion when the subject tries to communicate his knowledge to other rational beings and they either cannot understand it or deny its truth. It is important to remember that what *must* be the case in order for a judgement to be held by conviction is "the *possibility* of communicating it *and* of finding it valid for all reasoning beings."[19] If Winston runs into no rational beings who will communicate with him—a highly likely possibility in his situation—he is unlikely to discover that he is merely persuaded. (Here we see the limitation Kant would see as belonging to pragmatism: because no other person has communicated otherwise to us, we cannot infer that our propositions are true.) It is possible insofar as there is any rationality left in him, that Winston could discover that he is merely persuaded on his own, but this possibility requires that he utilize what is left of his rational capacities, a quite unlikely possibility. Something like 2+2=5, while communicable, is not able to be found valid by all reasoning beings. Someone could be persuaded of such a statement, but never convinced of it.[20] I suppose that the well-tossed word salad of a hebephrenic would be an example of a judgement(?) that is not possibly communicable and therefore fails the first test for conviction. The second test (universal validity) is obviously mooted in such a case.

Science is the building up of a system of conviction. Kant's resolution of the antinomies points out that empirical science is possible only under two premises: 1) that what is given (the objects of science) is conditioned, 2) that all of the conditions of the given objects are not given, but the complete set of conditions is thought. Under these premises "a *regress* to the conditions, that is a continual empirical synthesis, on the side of the conditions ,is enjoined or *set as a task*, and *in this regress* there can be no lack of given conditions."[21]

That science really does have, even in our late age, the aim of a complete *Wissenschaft*—a desire to grasp the fullness of the conditions of what is—despite all the revolutions in theory and method between Kant's day and ours, might be indicated by the fact that there is one mode science does not express itself in, though romance, tragedy, comedy, and myth could all be found. That mode is irony. A science which expressed itself as irony would be—well, it wouldn't be science.[22]

Empirical science—tracing out the conditions of what appears within what appears—is an essential task for human beings. It is essential because, on the one hand, every human being is given objects in sense experience which can only be known as conditioned and are only known insofar as one knows their conditions. (Here Kant agrees with the empiricists.) On the other hand, every human being has *a priori* the idea that what is conditional depends on what is unconditional. (Here he does not.) It is this idea of reason which grants the task of empirical science its hope of completion, while the first fact denies that that complete *Wissenschaft* is at any time actual: the object we know is always conditioned. Since conviction is defined socially—though that sociality is grounded in *a priori* elements of Reason, science is not only an essential task, but a social one and necessarily both. The scientific enterprise does not, for all this, form a community on its own, but takes place within a pre-existing one. The conditioned social activity known as science depends upon an originary and unconditioned social activity— morality. But that remark belongs a bit further along.

Now the question is, if the task assigned us by one part of our nature is constantly deferred by another aspect of our nature, is it not the case that our hope for completion of the task—a hope which is built into the very nature of a task—is an illusion, perhaps the work of some evil genius who has twisted us in such a way that we are, each and every one of us, a useless passion?

Kant does not think so. In fact , he thinks that the disjunction between what pure reason sets as a theoretical task and what can be given as an object to the understanding is almost a proof of the goodness of the spirit who has turned us this way. His response to this question about the reasonableness of our hope in the task set by theoretical reason is a deferral. His deferral is historically inter- esting because, among other things, it is a complete inversion of the Platonic deferral: In Diotima's erotic understanding of knowledge a human being moves from wanting to help give birth to good souls (politics) through knowing true theories (speculative philosophy) to seeing Beauty as it is in itself. Kant's deferral relocates the steps on Diotima's ladder: the theoretical interest of reason indicates that there is a higher step—reason's purely practical interest, and it is by reference to this interest and its achievement that what looks to be an inadequacy and a reason for despair on the side of speculation can be reasonably understood as a design of hope. Kant's replacement of the *vita contemplativa* by the *vita activa*, his valorizing of the practical interests of man over his speculative interest, changed the path of philosophy despite the best efforts of Fichte, Schelling and

Hegel.

Now to return to a point skipped over a moment ago: in what sense does science depend on morality? In the "Canon of Pure Reason" Kant sets up an analogy between theoretical reason and practical reason—theoretical reason can come to conclusions about the existence of things from the fact that some other things happen. The justification for such conclusions is the law of nature. Similarly, practical reason comes to conclusions about the existence of things from the fact that some other things ought to happen. The justification for such conclusions is the law of morality.

It is, first of all, very strange that Kant should say that a law allows us to draw the conclusion "something is." Existence can never be the conclusion of an argument (unless, of course, it is given in one of the premisses, in which case the non-trivial conclusion does not regard the existence of a thing, but what kind of a thing it is which exists). Kant's answer to this problem follows the only line open to him—he "assume[s] (in the first *Critique*) that there really are pure moral laws which determine completely *a priori*" (A807/B835), which is yet another way of deferring the problem of hope to the practical philosophy where the assumption of the existence of pure moral laws will be made good.

A *Wissenschaft* would be a complete system of knowledge of what is. As such there are two philosophical problems underlying science; if they cannot be answered, then they undermine the project of science. If they can be answered, then what allows for the answer is what allows (is the grounds for the possibility of and provides the bounds for) the entire project. The two problems Kant sees underlying science are these: What is cannot be proven to be a unity *"in accordance with speculative principles of reason"* (A807/B835, Kant's emphases). A complete system of knowledge cannot ground itself. The second problem, not unrelated, is that "what is" is not all explainable via the same kind of principles. Rather, two different kinds of principles are needed, one set which relates what is to what does happen, and one which relates what is to what ought to happen, to use Kant's words (A807/B835). In order for knowledge to be unified these principles must be shown to have a certain relation— hierarchic, inherence, ground-consequent—at this point Kant would not be particular, but there must be some way to unify the two kinds of principle.

These two problems must be resolved or science is not knowledge, for unlike stories told for entertainment, an explanatory story is only as good as its weakest link. If an explanation is not complete, then it is really not an explanation, though in places it may be a very pretty story. Keats' equivalence relations do not hold in the realm of literature calling itself science. But (to continue with a metaphor Kant likes) if this province of literature and human endeavor is part of a kingdom ruled by principles whose source is a capital distinct from, though not at war with, the provincial capital of science, then it is by relationship to the greater kingdom that what goes on within the province of science is finally explainable. That the realm allows the provinces freedom means that each province sets up its own laws for what is to count as a good story within it. But the regulated freedom within the province is not the creation of the province, it holds by virtue of the principles held in the capital of the realm.

Kant's idea of what counts as explanation, as well as his ideas about the practice of morality are tied up with the idea of an essential task attributed to him in the first part of this chapter. Scientific explanation and the practice of virtue are what may be called extended actions. Unlike getting out of bed in the morning, an extended action is one which is not fully accomplished at any moment. Extended actions are the natural implication of an essential task. So too are encompassing passions. It is possible, for example, for a man to fall in love with a woman and though they never marry, perhaps rarely see each other, to love the woman throughout his life. Say he becomes an author. He writes every word for her—the extended action of his authorship, though made up of many acts, is really one act, the passions evoked, described, demythologized are all funded by one encompassing passion—love for her. Most lovers are more pragmatic—the world these days is complex and one life has many passions. But the practice of virtue and of science demands more of a person than a modern lover demands, at least on Kant's view. The good will demands that maxims not in accord with the categorical imperative not be taken up. It demands that desire be subjected to reason and the good will demands it constantly, bears it out even to the edge of doom. Where morality demands constancy, explanation demands completeness: local understandings are not sufficient. To explain y by references to x and then to say that x is radically inexplicable is to claim "dormitive virtue" for sleeping powders or to demand that lost little girls and scarecrows "pay no attention to the man behind the curtain." To obey such a command, or to disobey the categorical moral demand is to give up the task, the activity, and the passion. But if the task is essential, then to give it up is a way of attempting suicide.

As Kant understands it the only unity of the world is moral (A808/B836): the realm we communicate in is (always already) the ethical community.[23]   Whereas any particular scientific community *comes to be* via understanding the phenomena, a rational being thinks himself *already in* the moral community by virtue of the fact of being able to think his maxims as universally legislative in a kingdom of legislators. As a rational being I must think myself *already in* this community and act *from* it, where the scientific community is *built from* action in and on the world. The moral world is the world in which, as rational beings, we always already are. What Augustine says about finding out something we did not know fits here as an example of the relation Kant sees between the scientific enterprise and morality. "It [the discovery of something new] reveals the beauty of minds that have been brought together in fellowship ... through signs" (*DT* X.2). Our desire for knowledge is met by listening to and answering questions— including questions put to nature—through signs, but this signal activity reveals an already existing agreement and conjunction of free minds. That's the *beauty* of it. It is needless to remind anyone that for Augustine beauty is always more than just the *symbol* of the moral, but participates in the very being of the good.

Kant, perhaps, does not go quite so far as Augustine, for in places he seems to think morality is an *a priori capability* of, not necessarily an *actuality* for, every rational being in the world: we may be immoral and so freely opt out of that world—but then are we rational beings?[24] Scientific and metaphysical worlds may be destroyed, there may be revolutions—Copernican and otherwise— within the province of science, but the world all rational beings are in is one (true, beautiful, good ...). Practical conviction about this

possible experience of being part of a moral kingdom is achieved
when the maxim of my action matches the categorical imperative
(because only, and always, in such cases am I acting as a member
of that community). This kind of action is required of me because I
can think of myself as free; that is, I can think of myself as being
motivated solely by this conception—that the maxim of my action
can be willed simultaneously to be a universal law.[25]

Gilles Deleuze lately, and others (notably Hegel) earlier, take
this point of Kant's to be an inversion of the ancient philosophical
opinion. Deleuze says that whereas for Plato the law was "only a
'second resort', a representation of the Good in a world deserted by
the gods.... Kant reverses the relationship of the law and the
Good:.... It is the Good which depends on the law not vice versa"
(*Kant's Critical Philosophy*: x). This seems to me partly right and
partly wrong. The relationship between the right and the good is
rather more complex than Deleuze's phrasing lets on. To borrow the
language Kant uses to explain the relationship of the moral law and
freedom is appropriate here: As the moral law is the *ratio
cognescendi* of freedom and freedom the *ratio essendi* of the moral
law, so the moral law is the *ratio cognescendi* of the Good, and the
Good is the *ratio essendi* of the moral law. The moral law aims at
the unqualified good. This is exactly the relationship exhibited
between the law and the Good in the dialogue of *Republic*, where it is
only after imagining being raised according to the laws of reason
that Socrates is led to the question of the Good—a question which, let
it be remembered, he can only answer in images because he is as yet
in the land where law is all we can *know* of the Good. That land is
ours. The agreement of Hegel, Deleuze and other writers in their

criticism of Kant is linked to a second, also mistaken, criticism of Kant's moral philosophy, namely that it is an empty formalism. That Kant does not define the moral good except by lawfulness, thus leaving "a form with no purpose," stems from the important fact that every finite good is a *finite* good. That is, a conditional one. As finite rational creatures we are always entwined in a world of finite goods, and precisely there is the moral danger—the danger of a mistake in judgement about which finite good in our particular situation is the good to be aimed at. Only a formal criterion is possible here—unless (*per impossible*) the Good should show up in its entirety in the finite. No measure of finite goods, such as in utilitarianism or any socialism—even if possible—can get the answer we *need* here, for what morality aims at is not a finite good, nor even the world of them. Morality aims at the Good. What profit would there be to gain the whole world but lose that? The moral law is the *ratio cognescendi* of the Good for life in the cave, for those who "here live by faith".

When St. Bonaventure wrote his little treatise, *De Reductione Artium ad Theologiam*, he did not reduce the arts to something less than what they are in themselves, but exhibited their openness to something far greater. So, too, here: Morality, whose concept—freedom, and whose command—duty, transcends but does not contradict the legitimate uses of all the concepts of the understanding, is because of that transcendence the queen of the sciences, the capital of the realm of Reason.[26] Every empirical science, every speculative enterprise, is part of a world which is primordially moral. This moral unity of the world is not an objective reality—an object of intuition, but it is a necessary object of reason, and therefore, for the will, for practical reason, it is an objective reality.[27] It is the distinction between these two kinds of objective reality that "makes room for faith," and displaces the interest of speculative reason into the practical realm.

How the Answer Is Deferred

We cannot quite leave Kant's speculative philosophy yet, for not only does theoretical reason have something at stake—a unified world, which is the *telos* of its endeavor—but the arguments for hope have both a theoretical and a practical side. Like his arguments for freedom, the theoretical argument is negative, the practical one positive. To recall the distinction succinctly: From the negative point of view, freedom means independence from causality through sense. From the positive point of view, freedom is the power to act according to a law of one's own making from a purely rational (*a priori*) motive (A533f/B5621f; *FMM*: 4476f; *KPV*: 34). Speculative reason cannot disprove the existence of freedom, practical reason gives an analysis which serves as a deduction of its existence.

The negative definition of freedom is rather weak and must be true for any being which acts according to conceptions. The claim here is that while the human will is "*pathologically affected* by sensuous motives," that does not imply that it is "pathologically *necessitated*" (A534/B562). The claim of necessity is an *a priori* one for Kant, and since all of empirical science is based on, but does not discover or deduce *a priori* categories, no science can make or prove a claim of absolute (in the Hegelian sense) necessity. Thus the question of freedom can not be resolved by theoretical reason. Understanding is not competent to sit on the question. A being which acts according to conceptions is not necessitated by sense because concepts are not sensations. Conceptualizing immediately creates plurality, or at least duality. For example, a hungry conceptualizing being, when it sees something edible, may not just respond to the stimulus as a non-conceptualizing being does, but may first form a conception, such as "I can eat this to assuage my hunger." But the other side is immediately possible: "or I can not eat." Where it is possible to act, it is possible also not to act. As Aristotle points out, this kind of negative capability is necessary for there to be any grounds for praise or blame.

The positive definition of freedom—the capacity to be determined by reason alone—is what separates Kant's strict sense of morality and the practical from the theoretical and allows for the possibility of a metaphysics of morals. If freedom did not also have this significance, morality would not be different from what Kant calls the technically practical. Aristotle's ethics, he would say, is a system of this type, but not a moral system in Kant's strict sense. The positive sense of practical freedom is transcendental for the understanding, therefore the question of freedom, which theoretical reason was incapable of resolving, when affirmed by practical reason adds nothing to the realm of speculation. Since we can act according to a conception of ourselves as free beings, that is, as beings for whom there is a categorical imperative, we are for all practical purposes free. Freedom is thus a strange fact, for although it is an idea of reason, not an object of possible intuition, it is yet an idea on account of which things can be made to happen in the world of sense. Freedom has this strange combination of moeities: It is the only conception completely unintuitable which has effects which are intuitable.

It is by analogy with these two kinds of arguments that we can examine Kant's arguments for hope. There is a negative side: that understanding can give no decisive argument against hope. And there is a positive side: that what understanding is incompetent to resolve, reason answers affirmatively, yet without adding anything to the realm of speculation.

Kant himself points to the analogy between the negative definition of and argument for practical freedom and his negative argument for hope; in addition, the arguments are found in similarly titled sections of the two *Critiques*, the former in "The Solution of the Cosmological Idea of Totality" in the "Antinomy of Pure Reason," and the latter in "The Critical Resolution of the Antinomy of Practical Reason."28

Given that a finite rational being has a complex view of happiness which includes both sensuous and rational aspects and given the deferral of the ends of understanding and its laws to practical reason defended earlier in this chapter, the only way to organize the complex happiness required by a sensible being for whom reason alone can be practical is by understanding moral goodness—the consciousness of which leads directly to the moral part of happiness—as cause of sensible or physical happiness as well. We are justified in using understanding's category "cause and effect" rather than subtance/accident or any other dynamical category here because it is clear that the will does have causality in the sensible world. It is perfectly clear because that is what it means to act freely—to act according to a pure conception. Whether understanding can grasp what the will is and how it comes to do what it does or not is not an important issue here.

But once given this seeming foothold, understanding tries to "go further." It finds within itself no necessary (i.e., *a priori*) connection between the moral law and what occurs in nature. In fact, effects are not at all dependent upon the morality of intentions, but on the laws of physics.[29] Besides this denial of a connection between morality and desert, the slings and arrows of outrageous fortune seem to do nothing for our hopes but by opposing end them. For,

> take the case of a righteous man, ... [whose] will is disinterestedly to establish only that good to which the holy law directs all his energies. But he is circumscribed in his endeavor. He may, it is true, expect to find a chance concurrence now and again, but he can never expect to find in nature a uniform agreement—a consistent agreement according to fixed rules, answering to what his maxims are and must be subjectively, with that end which yet he feels himself obliged and urged to realize. Deceit, violence, and envy will always be rife around him, although he himself is honest, peaceable and benevolent; and the other righteous men that he meets in the world, no matter how deserving they may be of happiness, will be subjected by nature, which takes no heed of such deserts, to all the evils of want, disease, and untimely death, just as are the other animals on the earth. And so it will continue to be until one wide grave engulfs them all—just and unjust, there is no distinction in the grave—and

> hurls them back into the abyss of the aimless chaos of
> matter from which they were taken—they that were
> able to believe themselves the final end of creation.
> —Thus the end which this right-minded man would
> have, and ought to have, in view of his pursuit of the
> moral law, would certainly have to be abandoned by
> him as impossible (*KU* Section 87, 452).

In short, understanding finds that there is not only neither a pure
nor empirical connection between morality and happiness, but that
there also seems to be good empirical evidence against such a
connection. Therefore hope is unreasonable.

Kant's response is perfectly cogent given what we have seen of
the critical project: Understanding's *a priori* laws constitute all our
possible experience as finite rational beings with sensible intuition,
but what it is possible for understanding to know is, therefore, not
everything that is absolutely possible. Whatever unfolds in
experience is conditioned, therefore all empirical arguments
against hope are only conditionally true. The unconditional and
unconditioned cause of experience cannot even be made sense of by
understanding, much less appear within its realm. So, "it is not
impossible that the morality of intention should have a necessary
relation as cause to happiness as an effect in the sensuous world"
(*KPV*: 116).[30] If it does have such a relation, the truth of that relation
cannot be scrutable to understanding. Furthermore, since this hope
of our final end is a conception of our practical reason, it can
neither be inferred from any data of experience, nor disconfirmed
by it.[31] The slings and arrows argument cannot be used against

hope any more than the occasional poetic justice of the world can be used to support it. Any argument about the grounds, necessity, or irrationality of hope must be worked out from the standpoint of practical reason. All other standpoints transcend our rational, but finite, place. So not only is the end hoped for by theoretical reason deferred to the practical realm, but all positive arguments for it are also deferred to morality.

Chapter 2:

IS HOPE REASONABLE?

I: The Positive Arguments for Hope

> When the beginning is what one doesn't know, and
> the end and what comes between are woven out of
> what isn't known, what contrivance is there for ever
> turning such an agreement into knowledge?
>
> ——*Republic* 533c

Hope, which is at once both a theoretical and a practical issue, unites

the essential ends of human reason and thus unites philosophy,

which has two objects—nature and freedom. But Kant's arguments

for hope do not unite the ends of human reason into a speculative

system, rather a practical one. He has good reason to think that a

unity based on morality is the only legitimate system: 1) As finite,

needy beings we seek happiness (we are subject, by the fact of our

sensibility, to an assertoric imperative)[1] 2) As rational beings we

seek worthiness (we are subject to a categorical imperative). 3) The

unity of the two ends which we all share is the complete good. 4)

Furthermore, an impartial rational being (which standpoint each of

us can take, even with regard to ourselves) can only be pleased by

linking these two ends proportionally. 5) The idea of achieving the

complete good presents us with the idea of a world in which the laws

of efficient causality in nature would be set up according to a moral

purpose; that is, Nature's organization would be founded on a final

causality. 6) This idea of a *nexus finalis*, which is a creation of

pure reason, is a subjectively valid maxim for the investigation of

nature. (Were this idea of a *nexus finalis* objectively valid a transcendental justification of it would be both possible and required, but then aesthetic judgements would not be judgements of taste, rather judgements of Reason open to dispute and decidable by proofs.) 7) No matter what progress we make in the efficient causal explanation of nature, even if it extends (*per impossible*—since efficiency does not grasp the whole as a whole) to the whole of nature, the principle of final causality will remain a valid principle for reflective judgement. 8) The only way of thinking the unity of both systems of causes without destroying either efficient or final causal *nexus* is by thinking the mechanism of efficient causes as subordinate to the *nexus finalis*. 9) Since Reason requires both principles (understanding requires efficient causality, reason uses final causality), we must subordinate mechanism to a teleological principle,[2] or in other words we must subordinate theory to praxis, the speculative system to the practical employment of reason (which was the point this long chain of reasoning set as its *telos* at the beginning of this paragraph).

A second way to understand Kant's argument thus far is by analogy to Gödel's proof in number theory. In Kant's philosophy there are two models for reality. One, that of understanding, is incomplete, but proven (transcendentally) to be fully consistent. The second model, that of reason, is the complete model, but its consistency cannot be proven (nor disproven) by understanding. This second model includes the partial model of the understanding, but in addition affirms freedom and the moral law. As in number theory, knowledge—what understanding gets—of the consistency of the complete model is denied, and not merely in fact, but even as a possibility. It is the fact of freedom that gives the ability to prove the consistency of the first model,[3] but that fact is not modelled within

the system of understanding. Freedom remains, for understanding, a proposition the affirmation or denial of which are both
consistent with understanding's model of reality. For arithmetic
the undecidable formula (the Gödel sentence σ) is provable in the
metalanguage. In the same way Kant holds that freedom—the
undecidable proposition for speculation—is the fact upon which
morality is founded. The categorical imperative of practical reason
implies (and is implied by) freedom. The positive argument that
reason presents for hope begins precisely at this point where
understanding cannot hope to gain a foothold.

The Unity of the Ends of a Finite Rational Will

Freedom is a queer kind of fact in Kant's philosophy. Every
other fact is known through understanding and is discoverable in
intuition, but the way we know freedom is through the moral law
(*KPV*: 5n) which is the work of pure reason. The necessity of the
moral law allows reason to assert freedom, where understanding—
for which there can be no possible experience of the moral law—
could only allow freedom as possible. The assertion of freedom by
reason raises freedom's modal status above that of the other two
postulates—God and immortality—and gives the argument for those
two further postulates a practical footing.

All action is for an end; ends are objects of a will (Reason
functioning practically), not an understanding (Reason functioning speculatively). An end is therefore an element in a *nexus
finalis*, not an element in a chain of efficient causality. Any
rational will has goodness as its end—acting according to the idea
of lawfulness. Any finite rational will has, in addition, the end of

happiness, understood as "the satisfaction of all its desires" (A806/B834). These desires will be empirically discovered and differ, perhaps widely, from one species of rational will to another, and perhaps even within cultures of a single species. Nonetheless both ends will be necessary ends for the finite rational being, though the second end is difficult to pin down since 1) happiness is an ideal of imagination, not reason (i.e., we do not know how to connect all of our desires) and 2) what counts as an element of that happiness will vary widely from one rational being to the next insofar as each may have different desires.

The first positive argument for hope is based upon these facts about a finite rational will, and is repeated several times by Kant: The moral law and its end are apodictic practical imperatives applicable to all rational beings, though *imperative* only for those who are finite. There is also an assertoric practical imperative to which each finite rational will is bound. The first imperative with its end—morality—presents itself as having a dignity and as being an object of immediate respect (*FMM*: 411, 435f), that is, as an end in itself. The only systematic unity of the two ends is therefore one in which morality dictates to happiness, not the converse. Were the converse true, morality would have only a market price, measured by its achievement of happiness: It would not be an end in itself. Since as finite rational beings we have both ends—one by absolute necessity, the other by necessity of our nature—we must hope in and through our moral activity to achieve that state of affairs in which happiness is measured out according to morality. This hope requires God and immortality as principles for the achievement of the end. Since anyone who wills an end necessarily wills the means necessary for the achievement of that end, any finite rational being wills that there be a God and an eternal life whenever he is acting morally. This argument can be seen to depend upon a systematic demand for the unity of the finite rational will.

The Autonomy of Reason

A second argument is based on a demand for the autonomy of Reason. What Kant thinks is his main discovery, certainly what he sees as the center and impetus of the critical project, lies here: Reason constantly falls into dialectical contradictions by attempting to ascend to the absolutely unconditioned (*Letters*, to Garve; Sept. 21, 1798 and Aug. 7, 1783). The first step in resolving this scandal of the ostensible self-contradictions within Reason is to try to understand how they are possible. Reason's self-contradictions are attempts to say yes and no to the same thing. In order for these self-contradictions to be merely ostensible, not real, it must be the case that Reason is referring to two different objects or has two different approaches to one object, which objects or approaches it is mistaking as the same. Kant's explanation is that Reason necessarily postulates God, freedom and immortality on practical grounds and then attempts on theoretical grounds to prove both their existence and nature.

However, objects which are postulates of practical reason are not the same thing as objects for speculative reason, which are one and all things able to be given as objects of sensible intuition. The objects which are postulates of practical reason are, on the contrary, not objects of intuition, but projects of the will. (Schopenhauer saw this point, but then promptly lost the other side of the distinction—that objects of intuition are not knowable *as* projects of will—except, of

course, insofar as they are projects of one's own will.) The
contradictions Reason falls into are based, therefore, upon mistaking projects of the will for objects of the understanding and
attempting to treat them as such. By showing understanding its
proper objects we explain how the error was possible and though we
do not thereby rid ourselves of the temptation to it we gain a
discipline—custody of the eyes—to control it. Pure practical reason,
on the other hand, has its projects which account for "our inextin-
guishable desire to find firm footing somewhere beyond the limits of
experience" (A797/B825). If it were not possible for Reason to
account for its own seeming self-contradictions, it would have to be
the case that we have a desire for knowledge that is not rooted
anywhere within Reason. This option Kant believes to be absurd
since if it were the case that there were not a Rational ground for
those problem-causing ideas of Reason, it would be the case that
Reason was heteronomous—its highest objects, God, freedom and
immortality, presented to it by another source. Such a source, since
it would not have a Rational explanation, would make Reason's
basis something non-Rational. In brief, the ideas of God, freedom
and immortality, around which Reason's antinomies revolve, must
have their source in Reason and the seeming contradictions are
thus based in Reason or else Reason can make no claim justifying
itself as a source of knowledge for two reasons. First, since Reason
would rest upon something else, its justification would depend upon
that other thing. Secondly, since it leads itself into contradictions,
if it cannot explain away those contradictions on its own terms
Reason would be proven to be a useless tool. The critical project tries
to show that it is a part of being rational to have the ideas of God,
freedom and immortality and that it is because of having an

understanding which is linked to sensuous intuition that these ideas are only postulates and lead speculative Reason into antinomies. Thus Reason is defended, the postulates are necessary, and the hope based upon the postulates is eminently rational.

The Unity of the World

The third positive argument for hope is based upon a systematic demand for the unity of the world. This comes very close to being the same thing as a demand for the unity of ends of Reason, but it comes to it aiming in Reason's other direction: toward speculation. As rational beings with an understanding bounded by sense we experience everything as related through efficient causality. As we have already seen, we are never really given "everything"—the world in its entirety as efficiently caused—but as rational beings we can think everything as related through final causality. In such a *nexus finalis* the connection between happiness and worthiness would be necessary. However, since our world is one in which both 1) moral intentions are not scrutable, so we cannot see if or how they are causes and 2) not everyone does as they ought and so a unified moral world is not being visibly brought about, this necessary connection cannot be known to us. We can, however, *believe* it to be the case through a Supreme Reason who is Author and Moral Ruler of the world. Kant believes, though I have never seen him argue the case, that only if there is one unified world can the world be intelligible. This is clearly the classical philosophical position. Kant is, however, arguing against the tradition, when he claims that that unity is a *project* for rational activity, not a *factum* for speculation. He clearly believes that chains of efficient causality never achieve ordered wholeness, they merely lead from one thing to another *ad infinitum* in a mathematical series. The idea of the world as a whole is an idea of practical reason and it is under the rule and within the context of reason's (dynamical) project of one moral world that the efficient causal explanations make sense. But that the world is so unified and really intelligible to understanding is something we can hope for only under the postulates of a Supreme Reason who is Author and Ruler of it.

This last argument, based on Reason's requirement that the world be unified, as well as the first, based on the unity of the self, are the bases for two forms of praxis in the world, though neither can ever be established according to the discipline of speculative reason. The idea of the unity of the world is a *sine qua non* for empirical investigation; the idea of a complete good (and therefore a unified self) is the *sine qua non* for moral activity. Moreover, according to the second argument, the postulates *must* be thought or Reason has no autonomous foundation. It is therefore an "inner practical necessity" of Reason which leads outward to those postulates (A819/B847). It should now be clear how the question of hope unites all of the interests—speculative and practical—of our Reason.

If one looks at each of these three sources of the postulates of reason individually: the demand for unity of the finite rational will (happiness and worthiness), the demand for an autonomous foundation of Reason (an immanent source for its unmeetable speculative desires), and the necessity for a unity of the natural and moral worlds in both of which Reason and the self are found, the arguments seem weak, but the three support each other as well as the postulates of God and immortality in a way which makes the whole much more reasonable than the pieces seem at first sight. It is often thought, for example, that Kant's argument conjoining happiness and worthiness vitiates his moral philosophy, and in fact is unworthy of his own best insights.[4] But we can see from this perspective that such arguments are bogus. That moral virtue necessarily achieves a part of happiness (i.e., that part which a moral being achieves by acting in accord with reason) does not imply that virtue's motive is happiness. Moreover, the moral theory stands untainted by the necessity of aiming at a complete good which includes happiness, for it is another motive—unity of the human self—which brings in the requirement of happiness. This demand hangs together with the moral philosophy because if there were not a division in the self the moral law would not be experienced as an *imperative*. That the moral law is experienced as an imperative points to the fact of a division in the self: If we were not moved by purposes other than morality, morality would be a law like gravity rather than an imperative. That it is an imperative indicates that our heart is divided against itself. The conjunction of worthiness and happiness is required for the real *unity* of the self which is so divided.

Paralleling this argument is the fact that the natural world has laws according to which things happen, which laws are verified in experience, while the moral world has laws according to which things ought to happen. If these latter laws were, as well, verifiable in experience, the moral unity of the world would not need to be held as a postulate. And if this were the case we would perforce be moral, since assertoric and categorical imperatives would not only command the same thing but *be* the same thing. The only vice possible would be ignorance.

Finally, if we could *experience* the moral unity of the world
there would never have been a dialectic in Reason, for the
knowledge postulated and desired because of Reason's practical
employment would always already have been available
speculatively. Obviously, such is not the case, but the important
point is that the distinctions Kant has made allow the only
explanation to the question *why* it is not. And there may be some
truth to his claim that he is the first to show why philosophy has
continually had to begin again: so long as the moral unity of the
world is a hope, a speculative unity is a chimera.

The usual way of commenting upon Kant (cf. Beck, *Commentary*: 264-281) would note both that these three arguments are
practical reason's explanations of the sources of (respectively) the
ideal, the paralogisms and the antinomy of pure reason and that in
the work of the second *Critique* they raise the ideas of God, the soul
and the world to the level of postulates. Such remarks have
something to be said for them, but it seems to me that the arguments
for the unity of the ends of reason (which for speculation are an
ideal), for the autonomy of reason (which for speculation depends
upon paralogism) and for the unity of the world (which leads
speculation into its antinomies) are not only interdependent, but
also interwoven—the "practical proof" for God cannot be separated
from that for immortality or the unity of the world, and so also with
the unity of the world and immortality with each of their others.
Beck points this out after a fashion by noting that his restatements of
Kant's arguments (e.g., for immortality on page 269) "presuppose
the existence of God." The disadvantage of pulling the argument

into pieces which it is not in in Kant is that when the next argument defends the belief in the existence of God it looks as if Kant is arguing in a circle. Instead of that approach I have shown what motivates Kant's arguments for the postulates and that those motives are themselves intrinsically related. The arguments are not made more understandable by separating them.

In summary then, happiness and virtue are different things, irreducible the one to the other since both are ends for the finite rational self because of differing necessities of that self's existence. Since these two ends exist in the same being they must be able to be thought as systematically connected, but given that we come to know the good via the pure practical law (not vice versa) the rational will under the conditions of sensibility must link virtue to happiness as cause to effect (rather than the reverse) if it is to link them at all.

We have seen that it is impossible that evidence either against or for this link ever be available to speculative reason, since, among other reasons, virtue—even one's own—as the activity of the free will, is an unintuitable *causa noumenon*. The conclusion—that only an omnipotent rational will could create the necessary link between virtue and happiness—is important for three systematic reasons: First, the unity of the self. The hope for a unified self requires the postulate of God's existence—only he can connect the two ends of the rational self systematically. Secondly, something bigger, if not more important is at stake: The world, whether it shall be a universe or chaos.

> [R]eason does indeed have causality in respect of
> freedom in general, [though] it does not have

causality in respect of nature as a whole; and
although moral principles of reason can indeed give
rise to free actions, they cannot give rise to laws of
nature.... [Therefore, if there is to be a systematic
unity of nature, it] cannot be proved *in accordance
with speculative principles of reason* (A807/B835).

The world, therefore, must be a moral world, a world that has
objective reality in that each rational being in its own moral action
views the sensible world of efficient causality as subject to a moral
unity of final causality. Finally, if Reason is to be autonomous and
justify itself as a faculty of knowledge, it must define its own ends
and give an explanation for its seeming contradictions. That God,
the moral world and freedom are postulates of practical reason
unavailable as objects to speculation guarantees Reason as both
autonomous and coherent. It is only because all these practical
postulates are accepted that the world is knowable and morality is
non-suicidal. And so these arguments reflect back onto the kind of
self whose possibility is being outlined here, for according to Kant if
objective knowledge is to be possible at all, if our action is not to be
absurd, immoral, or at best tragic, and if this Rational self is to be
one thing, God must be postulated. But if everything so depends upon
God, is Kant telling the same kind of story that it seemed he started
out to tell? It is Kierkegaard, not Kant, who writes "man's need of
God is his highest perfection" (*ED*: 136).

II: The Paradoxes of Hoping

> It is a highly unphilosophical expedient to resort to a
> number of proofs for one and the same proposition,
> consoling oneself that the number of arguments
> makes up for the inadequacy of any one of them
> taken by itself; for this bespeaks cunning and a lack
> of sincerity.
>
> ——Immanuel Kant

One way to read the first *Critique* and *Prolegomena* is as a kind of
spiritual exercises, for their aim is to discipline Reason. Within
the bounds of sense Reason legislates over objects making
knowledge of them possible—the synthesis of imagination is subject
to Reason's categories and through these categories the objects are
known. Outside the bounds of sense... But a transcendental
deduction is also outside the bounds of sense. Kant's philosophy has
three such deductions, no two of them alike in all ways. What they
all share—besides the fact that they are acts of Reason not tied to the
synthesis of imagination—are three things: First, they are all
immanent; that is to say, the power of Reason which is being called
into court gives its own defense and exhibits its own particular
power in its defense. Secondly, each deduction must prove the
necessity of the rule it is defending. Third, each must also exhibit
the *universality* of its rule. The last two are what Kant would
consider the truth conditions of the critical philosophy.[5] That is, if
he can prove both, then the critical philosophy is true. Kant's
writing of the *Critiques* is his attempt to exhibit the universality of
the rule grounding each power, and in that enterprise he looks to his
reader "for the patience and impartiality of a judge" (A xxii).

As judges our attention is directed to the second item—the

necessity claimed in each deduction, and so our assent to the argument presented for necessity of the rule in question in each *Critique*—the assent of each judge guided by his own Reason—will exhibit, insofar as that is possible, the universality which the theoretical discipline, the practical purposiveness, and the act of judgement require if the *Critiques* are to count as true and knowledge even though they are not connected to possible intuitions in the synthesis of imagination.   The dialectic of the truth conditions in Kant's arguments is thus self-consciously grounded in part on rhetoric: universal persuasion of his judges is a necessary, though not sufficient, condition for the critical philosophy to count as true. If rational beings can understand the dialectic of the argument without agreeing to it, then the argument is a failure, even though it be dialectically flawless. The twin demands of universality and necessity are therefore separable: the proof of the latter is not the same thing as the proof of the former. Kant, of course, does not believe that a failure in the one condition (universality), given the other (necessity), is a real possibility since what the critical philosophy gives are the conditions for the possibility of a community of rational beings, and this community is a fact since we have science, literature, laws, symbolic communicative activity. Thus in order for the dialectic of the argument to be meaningful it seems that the rhetorical point must already have been granted. By this means rhetorical conviction is wholly incorporated into dialectic (using the terms rhetoric and dialectic in Aristotle's sense, not Kant's) and mere persuasion is placed wholly outside the bounds of the meaningful.[6]

It remains to us, as judges, to investigate the Kantian claim that the moral unity of the world is a necessary object of Reason. We can summarize Kant's argument in terms that exhibit its modal character more clearly:

1. The moral end (worthiness) is necessary.

2. The moral end must connect with all other ends of Reason. (It is not possible to think that the moral end does not connect with all other ends of Reason.)

3. It is not possible to know of any other way to connect the moral end with all other ends of Reason except through an Author and Ruler of the two worlds.

4. It is not possible to know that God and a future life are impossible.

5. Belief in God and a future life is left open by theoretical reason and required by practical reason.

The necessity spoken of in premise 1 is purely practical necessity. Kant's argument for this premise ranges through two texts, the *Foundations* and *Critique of Practical Reason*. In the first section of the *Foundations* he sifts all the possible candidates for intrinsic value and after the process there remains only one thing— sparkling like a jewel by its own light: the good will. In fact "this end shines so as an ideal that it seems, by human standards, to eclipse holiness itself" (*DV*: 396). The center of the good will—"that which is connected with [it] merely as ground and not as consequence" (*FMM*: 400)—is duty, and duty alone can be (since it is the ground of the will and not consequence) "an object of respect, and thus an imperative" rather than a object of inclination and merely subjunctive. The good will is an object of respect for reason because it is a purpose determined by reason. In the second section of the *Foundations* Kant points out the implication of this discovery of the will as the locus of intrinsic value, and duty as its center: "The pure conception of duty ... has an influence on the human heart so much more powerful than all other incentives ... that reason ... despises them and ...thereby first realizes that it can of itself be practical" (*FMM*:411).

The realization there remarked upon becomes the object of a transcendental analysis in the second *Critique*. There Kant shows that the law of practical reason (as the categories of theoretical reason) cannot rest upon any principle of sense or inclination, for these would only be general, not—as Reason demands—universal and necessary. Thus the consciousness of duty evoked in the *Foundations* is shown, in the second *Critique*, to be consciousness of freedom of the will, the "consciousness of existence as determinable in an intelligible order of things" (*KPV*: 43). "Thus freedom and unconditional practical law reciprocally imply each other" and the former is known through the latter as its only possible ground (*KPV*: 30).

The second premise has a necessity that is both practical and theoretical. It is practical in that a limited rational being has other ends than the moral end necessarily, though those ends are not necessary in the same way, for at least some of those practical necessities are not commanded by reason purely.[7] It is theoretical in that since Reason is the ability to unite under principles, to deny that Reason can unite its own ends under principles is to deny that reason can do what it does. Kant believes that if our Reason could not unify its own ends the very act of Reasoning would be impossible. Since all Reasoning is unifying under principles and acting is bringing ends into existence, acts of Reason as well as reasoned actions assume this premise necessarily. As we have seen, in order to do science—in order to begin to trace the causal chain of conditions—we must have the idea (and the hope) of one whole—a world—the sum total of the conditions.

The third premise: the impossibility of knowing any other way to connect moral and natural ends is due to the limitations that the first *Critique* placed on theoretical reason. Therefore the requirement of God and a future life is one of practical necessity, or, as Kant says, they are moral beliefs. It would be a modal mistake to think that the practical necessities of the premises allowed a theoretically necessary conclusion. Against this Kant always says that practical reason does not enlarge the theoretical realm. Nevertheless, there does seem to be a theoretical necessity behind positing eternal life and a moral ruler of the world, for we have seen that theoretical reason cannot even get a start without the idea and hope of a unified whole of causal relations. We cannot, however, ever have an intuition of such a whole. But it is not enough that theoretical reason requires the idea of a world. As the *telos* of theoretical reason it is a pure creation of Reason which can never attain to the level of knowledge. What saves the idea of the moral unity of the world from being mere dogmatic opinion is the fact of the categorical imperative on the practical side. This fact lends to the idea a kind of necessity and a kind of truth that no other mere *ens rationis* can claim: practical necessity, practical (moral) proof.

What is the nature of this practical necessity, specifically with regard to the second premise, which the third *Critique* is at pains to show has objective analogues, though not objective (thus theoretical) intuitions or proofs? How does the fact of a categorical imperative redeem the idea of a moral world order from being a mere *ens rationis*? There is a practical rule of skill which says that where one wills the end one wills the means. But this rule is for ends within our power. If, for example, I had said to Kant "I will travel from Königsberg to Paris this afternoon and have supper in the garden behind the apse of Notre Dame," he would have said "no you don't" because the means for doing so were not discoverable in nature in his day. Since willing the end implies willing the means and the means are non-existent, willing the end is impossible. He would have called it a mere wish (bloßer Wunsch) to travel from Königsberg to Paris in an afternoon. The practical proposition "I will have supper in Paris today" implies the theoretical proposition (granted that I say it to Kant in Königsberg at lunch) "there is an available means to travel from Königsberg to Paris in an afternoon." Kant knows the theoretical proposition to be false, hence the practical proposition is a mere wish.

Kant's "moral proof" takes advantage of the fact that the parallel is not quite true when we transfer this line of reasoning from the technically practical to the purely practical. I am commanded to achieve the complete good; I make this the maxim of my will. Neither Kant nor I can know that the theoretical proposition implied in my act of will (there is a God and a future life which make that end possible of achievement) is false. Hence I am justified in believing it true, and justified on rational grounds. Our Reason requires a connection, practical reason requires the consequent, hence the ground is postulated. It should be clear how such a postulate is not an example of knowledge and so why practice gives no new grounds for speculation.

But there is another difference between the cases of the technically practical and the morally practical. The second difference is that, unlike a question of travel from Königsberg to Paris, the end of a moral world order is not wholly within our power, though part of it is—I can (perhaps) make myself worthy to be a part of such an order. That part of the end is commanded and the means are available, even though my gifts be only the niggardly provision of a step-motherly nature. But if, as Kant admits, the Ideas of Reason "lead understanding, in its study of nature, according to a principle of completeness, *unattainable as this remains* for it, and so promote(s) the ultimate aim of all knowledge," (*KU*: 168, emphasis added) why is it that in the moral sphere we must assume that what these ideas present *is* attainable? The faculty of knowledge has its limits, suffers from incompleteness, so why should the faculty of desire not also have limits on its fulfillment, why should it not also suffer from incompleteness?

The problem may be given a more radical twist: Is it not possible that the Reason which presents this end to us is a genius no less malicious than powerful? Kant points out in the first *Critique* that it is Reason itself which leads into dialectical error. He shows how the demon works in the second half of that book (the "Transcendental Dialectic"). We cannot exorcise him in the theoretical sphere,[8] though we can dampen his effects. Just so, we cannot deny the attractiveness of the end he presents to our practical reason; but how do we know that reason is not here the same dialectical, malicious, powerful demon? The medieval answer was that the Truth (God) is index of itself and falsity, and that Reason is able to measure the truth is guaranteed by Truth itself—though it is so guaranteed only as long as Reason stands in true relation to the Truth. That true relation is faith. The pure faculty of desire does not have this guarantee, unless we take reason's (the demon's?) word that his purity guarantees his goodness. How do we *know* that this is not the promise of a snake, that the end presented by the pure faculty of desire is not a fruit delicious to look upon, but dangerous to partake of, and in fact a lie?

That we want it to be otherwise I do not deny. It is built into the word 'want' as both lack and desire, and want is built into a finite rational volition. Kant thinks that this want is a need and necessities must be practically filled. Against this there is the fact that sometimes practical necessities are not filled, and the needy being dies. (It is the blight man was born for.) Why, then, must we assume that the means for the fulfillment of Reason's moral demand is available here? Why can't we say that the highest end (the harmony of natural and moral worlds) is a mere wish? If our highest end were a mere wish—impossible to achieve—whatever it is that is the source of this wish could have no better name than evil genius. And if the wish were intrinsically necessary for us, so that we could not escape having it, then the genius would be one who is no less powerful than he is malicious. No exit.

Kant responds that morality is unconditionally commanded and that this unconditionality could only be so by virtue of being grounded in true goodness. To draw a parallel with Descartes here may make Kant's argument clearer. Descartes' argument for the existence of God in the third *Meditation* can only make sense by being an argument by exclusion set up on a trilemma: *Either* I am an infinitely potent being, *or* there is an infinitely potent and non-deceptive God, *or* there is an infinitely powerful deceiver. One of those explanations is needed because I have an idea of God as an infinitely potent being and every idea requires a cause that has at least as much formal reality as the idea has objective reality. The first is clearly false because I am aware of having been in error against my will; were I infinitely powerful that would not happen. The last must be false because the genius' power of deception is limited by my certain knowledge of my own existence when I say *"Cogito;"* the middle option must be true. Similarly, Kant sees three options: Either the moral law is invalid, or it is valid and possible of fulfillment, or it is valid but impossible of fulfillment (the command of an evil genius). It cannot be invalid since my idea of goodness is bound up with it. Without the moral law there would be nothing in the world that is good without qualification. Without something that is good without qualification we could have no measure for goodness—no primary *exemplum* in relation to which all other good things take their name. Good would collapse into useful, and without the goodness of a good will even the good of happiness is corrupted.

An argument against the last option is more complex. Since the moral law is discovered within as unconditionally laid upon me and since it is also unconditionally tied up with the very conception of the good, the question of a thoroughly evil genius laying this unconditional command upon me cannot even be thought coherently. An argument something like this protects us from the thought that practical reason could at its root be a dialectical demon. But morality is only one part of the highest good; it is what makes us worthy to partake of happiness (and no unworthies may enter here— except unhappily). Say that the moral end—worthiness—is both possible and necessary; it is within our reach. But does *pure* practical reason require a moral world order? No. Its requirement is simply that I make myself worthy to be a member of it. As Kant himself illustrates by his examples in the *Foundations* and explicates in the "Incentive of Pure Practical Reason"—I must follow my duty though it thwart all my inclinations. This incentive, this moral attraction of duty, since it is not pathological but purely practical, cannot be excised or changed except by loss of one's reason. Pure practical reason does not demand that all of our ends cohere, but that this one end be actualized: worthiness. There doesn't seem to be much argument for the necessity of the coherence of all our ends as yet. The *complete* good may be an idea given us by an evil genius.

In the third *Critique* Kant attempts to strengthen the defense of what I have called premise two, for he is quite aware of these demonic arguments and of the status of the character whose story the moral life is if those arguments are not frustrated: The moral man is a tragic hero who embodies the quintessential human flaw: two ends—morality and happiness—in living contradiction. *So leben wir*, with one end commanded while holding another, in actuality contradictory to the first, which we cannot give up.[9] Does our hope for a moral world—a world in which all the ends of Reason are united—have any objective ground or not?

> That [end] which we have seen
>
> may be a devil and the devil hath power
>
> T'assume a pleasing shape, yea, and perhaps
>
> Out of [our] very weakness and [our] melancholy,
>
> As he is very potent with such spirits,
>
> Abuses [us] to damn [us]. [We'll] have grounds
>
> More relative than this (*Hamlet* II, ii 584-590).

A. The (Non)Objectivity of Hope

1. The Problem of the "Deduction" in the Third *Critique*

The question about hope is both a question about the unity and autonomy of our Reason and also a question about the unity of our entire nature—Reason and feeling, active and passive powers. In order to defend his argument for hope Kant must be able to show that judgements which link Reason and feeling have an objective ground. If such an objective ground cannot be given, then the argument in defense of moral hope does not "tend toward conviction," but is mere persuasion. What is it, then, that grounds the possibility of such a judgement? This question is Kant's prime concern in the third *Critique*.

There seem to be only two choices: *Either* judgement has a rule it gives to itself *a priori*, by which it directs its activity, *or* judgement is a groundless leap. (Or, I should say, to give the metaphor something to stand on, a leap which can go in any direction—as Kant would say: judgement is heteronomously determined.) If the latter, then any aesthetic judgement can not only never claim to be true or valid for all, but, because of the infinite variability in the connection of our feelings to Reason, incommunicable as well. The case of aesthetic judgement is more problematic than exposing the "conditions for the possibility" of either other faculty because it is a capacity "of judging of forms without the aid of concepts, and of finding, in the mere estimate of them, a delight" (*KU*: 300). Since everything that is universally communicable is conceptual, as for example, concepts of both understanding and reason are, and feelings of delight are not, the only way such judgements can be communicable is if they can be shown to have an *a priori* principle of their own. A judgement of taste, then, exhibits the peculiar combination of being both non-conceptually based and linguistically communicable.[10]

Kant's grounding of the judgement of taste undergoes a devolution that looks completely different from the similarly named processes in the two previous critiques. In "The Deduction of Pure Aesthetic Judgements" (§§30-55), he successively labels his task deduction (§30), demonstration (§31), investigation (§34), and finally, assumption (§38). The differences between each step exhibit peculiarities of the judgements of taste that were not the case in judgements grounded in the *a priori* concepts of Reason.

A: Deduction

A deduction in either of the two earlier *Critiques* has two vectors, as each side of an arch would have two vectors. On both sides (understanding and reason) there is an anchoring vector, for the deduction grounds universal validity *a priori* of the categories (or universal principles) of nature or of freedom. There is as well a thrusting outward or centrifugal vector, for the necessity of the principle(s) being deduced is dependent on an *a priori* proof competent to enforce the assent of all other rational beings. In contrast, judgement, as the keystone, both is supported by (i.e. may be"annexed to" [KU: 168]) understanding and reason *and* supports the outward thrust of each (by giving a rule for how we link a particular representation either to understanding or to reason). In a determinant judgement, where the universal is given, judgement is used as an annex to the faculty supplying the concept. In a reflective judgement, where the particular is given, judgement must give a rule to itself determining how the representation given in imagination is to be unified with the cognitive power (either understanding or reason). But since judgement thereby does not legislate over objects (as both understanding and reason do), but rather over itself, no deduction of the principle of judgement is, strictly speaking, possible. Kant calls the faculty of Judgement's peculiar kind of legislation heautonomous. A faculty that is heautonomous can at most give a demonstration of its first principles.

B: Demonstration

A demonstration, in contrast to a deduction   a) is to ground universal validity *a priori* of a *singular* judgement and   b) has a necessity depending on no *a priori* proof capable of enforcing the assent of all (*KU*: §31). While the first element of a demonstration may be explicable, the second seems problematic, at least in Kant's terms—for if the necessity of these judgements is not *a priori*, it is empirical and empirical necessity decides questions of fact, but never questions of right. The critical philosophy is a thoroughgoing investigation, up until this point at any rate, of the right of certain concepts/judgements to perform the tasks they lay claim to. This is a large "logical peculiarity" of "this strange faculty," but fitting, for there could be no *a priori* proof of sensuous aspects of a Rational being. It may, however, yet be the case that this principle which is not provable via an *a priori* proof rests, nonetheless, on *a priori* grounds (*KU*: §31).

Before we continue with the peculiar devolution of this strange deduction however, it might be worthwhile to caricaturize what Kant avoids by attempting it. This will also tie us back to the epistemological problems mentioned in Chapter 1. The peculiarity of this book is due to the peculiarity of the subject matter, for pure judgements of taste are A) autonomous, universal (like other pure judgements) and non-conceptual (unlike other judgements). The second peculiarity (B) is their claim to *a priori* necessity without *a priori* proof. First (A), that a judgement is autonomous, universal and non-conceptual seems to make it incommunicable: try communicating non-conceptually to everyone. There are only three ways for a philosopher to deal with what is going on here:

1. An objectivism *a la Moore* claiming that there are simple unanalysable qualities of things, but with no help forthcoming to those poor blokes who don't see those qualities. Indeed, because they are unanalysable no help is possible for such beings. A second problem for Moore is that no two blokes who claim to see the same thing can talk about it to make sure either.

2. A radical subjectivism *a la* the French (Descartes to Sartre): every subject reconstitutes the world according to its own (free) mode of taking it in. Not much communication here either, but at least Sartre seems to avoid a moralizing distinction between the

"in" group and the "outs".

3. Some road less easily travelled whereby a thing is called "beautiful in respect of that quality in which it adapts itself to our mode of taking it in" (*KU*: 283).[11] A kind of subjectivism, to be sure, but one which, with a theory of human nature, could ground communication.

If you understand these choices and if these are the whole range, then it seems that *either* the first two must be wrong *or* have no story to tell about how your understanding of these choices is possible.

The rest of the story about judgements of taste (B, above), is their peculiar claim to *a priori* necessity independent of *a priori* proof, which was discussed briefly above. What is avoided by *a priori* necessity is purely empirical necessity—the kind Moore has in ethics, for example—which Kant says gives up both the claim to universal necessity (things could be otherwise for some blokes) and autonomy of the individual's taste—for what would count as beautiful is what got the votes of those in the know.

This problematic claim to *a priori* necessity without *a priori* proof, which comes about because *a priori* proofs must be wholly conceptual and judgements of taste are not, leads to the next step in the devolution of the deduction. Since the determining ground of a judgement of taste will not be a concept (not be objective), all that is left for investigation is the subject. The investigation of the subject will be at the same time, however, an investigation into the way *the object must* "adapt itself to our mode of taking it in." Thus there will still be necessity, albeit subjective, and although the investigation is into the subject, it is not completely on the Cartesian end of the epistemological hyperbola.

C: Investigation

In any experience the subject employs at least two faculties: imagination, which synthesizes the manifold temporally, (*KU*: 287) and understanding or reason, which provides a concept which represents the manifold as a unity. We can skip the latter combination (imagination linked with reason), since those judgements are either moral or sublime. We have no problems with cognitive judgements in which understanding gives a rule for synthesis to the imagination. We are left with those cases in which understanding and imagination are in non-directive interaction: free play. This free play can be experienced as pleasurable. To reflect upon this interaction of the faculties is to make a judgement of the beautiful. When a judgement of the beautiful claims universality it is claiming that this subjective condition is true for all subjects. This investigation of the possible links between our faculties is not a proof of the objectivity of aesthetic judgement, though it does rest upon *a priori* considerations: we have three faculties, two of which have been proven to legislate over objects *a priori*, there are only four possible combinations of those two faculties with the third: There are two kinds of determinative judgement in which either understanding or reason gives the rule to imagination; there are two kinds of aesthetic judgement in which understanding or reason is in free play with imagination (these latter are judgements of the beautiful and judgements of the sublime respectively).

D: Assumption

Before taking the next step one might want to ask why Kant thinks that judgements of the beautiful claim universality *a priori*. The answer is simply that he thinks there is a difference between Anchises' agreeable experience of Venus while on her mountain and the art lover's experience of Venus de Milo while at the Louvre. The first, as an immediate sensation about which each may dispute as to whether or not it is agreeable (Anchises might have preferred his sheep), *actually* joins a cognition with feeling; the second, as a reflective judgement (allowing contention, not dispute)[12] claims a *necessary* connection between cognition and feeling. This necessity "is exactly what makes an *a priori* principle apparent in their case [that of aesthetic judgements], and lifts them out of the sphere of empirical psychology" (*KU*: §29). In addition, since a judgement of the beautiful is reflective and *not merely sensible* it can make sense to require a similar judgement from others, whereas, in the first case (Anchises' judgement of the sensually agreeable) such a demand is nonsense—concerning taste in this literal sense there can be neither dispute nor contention.

It is clear that we do make judgements of the beautiful, moreover, that we do regard them as different from the agreeable; and since the previously defended transcendental logic gives Kant a ground for the difference in judgement we are justified in assuming the same subjective interplay and unity of abilities in all men. In addition, when a judgement pays regard merely to this "way of taking in the object" the judgement of that object as beautiful may rightly demand universal assent (*KU*: 290n).

2. What Does the Deduction Prove?

There are several important points that fall out of Kant's argument
in the third *Critique*: 1) on his explanation of the judgement of the
beautiful it is possible that every object, if one would pay attention
only to the interplay of the faculties set in motion, could be
considered beautiful, since everything that is an object for us must
"adapt itself to our mode of taking it in." This is as it should be
since the principle of judgement was expected to be "heautonomous,"
that is, (a) although the principle of judgement does not legislate
over a certain realm of objects as understanding's principles do
over nature, or reason's law over morals, (b) judgement does,
without reference to such principles find pleasure in a
representation (as reason does in the representation of an act done
from duty). 2) Aesthetic judgements are possible only for beings
with both passive and active faculties, e.g., beings with both
intuition and understanding. God's creative understanding is not
capable of such since it bestows existence, whereas aesthetic
judgements are disinterested—and "to will something, and to take
delight in its existence [is] to take an interest in it" (*KU*: §4). Or,
equivalently, by definition of "aesthetic," such judgements are only
possible for beings whose experience is spatio-temporal, i.e., beings
with sensuous intuition and, by definition of "judgement," aesthetic
judgements are only possible for Rational beings. 3) Since the
interplay of the imagination and either reason or understanding
that is the basis of the aesthetic judgement results in a feeling of
pleasure (in a judgement of the beautiful) or a kind of pain (in a
judgement of the sublime), it would seem that such judgements
could only be made by intuitive, Rational, embodied beings. An

angel, whatever that is, could never make them. Most importantly
(4), since judgement unites all our faculties together, a being with a
different form of intuition or a different kind of imagination or
understanding—if possible—(i.e., a different set of *a priori*
categories and forms of intuition) would have to have a different
principle of judgement for both types of aesthetic judgement. Were
those kinds of creature to exist we could not communicate with them,
nor they with us. We would not live in the same world. The
Critique of Judgement thus ends where the critical project began: It
concludes Kant's justification of his "Copernican revolution" in
which every philosophical question is "adapted to the human point
of view," with a thoroughly humanized theory of judgement (*KU*:
§76).

Does this devolved deduction, which shows how it is possible for
Reason and feeling to work together, give us true grounds to hope
that the ends of Reason and the end of inclination are able to meet in
the moral world where happiness accords with desert? That depends
on what you mean by true.

Kant's own story revolves around the faculty of judgement,
which stands—with freedom and hope—as central to the whole
critical project. In the first chapter we saw how hope is a question
which "is at once practical and theoretical." In the first part of this
chapter we saw how freedom, though never an intuition for
understanding, is nonetheless a fact for reason and therefore is a
one-way bridge from theoretical reason to practical reason.
Judgement, which "forms a middle term between reason and
understanding" (*KU*: 168, 177), in addition unites our active
Rational faculties directly with our passions—specifically the

capacity to feel pleasure and pain. We find by experience that there is such a connection, but Kant argues that it is an *a priori* one. We have just rehearsed how Kant argues for that *a priori* connection.

The third *Critique* does not succeed in giving *universal subjective validity*—i.e., in grounding conviction—for the principle of judgement. In acts of aesthetic judgement the subject claims universal validity for her judgement—and everyone, in making an aesthetic judgement, makes the same claim of universal validity. The worth of this *subjectively universal validity* of the principle of judgement seems to be grounded by some very fast hand waving at the transcendental logic. I have assumed all along that the first two critiques work, but perhaps it is not so. Nevertheless, continuing to assume that they do, in what way do they allow the claim that "since the transcendental logic gives a ground for the difference" between judgements of the agreeable and judgements of the beautiful, "we are justified in assuming the same subjective interplay and unity of abilities in all men"(see above)? The entire critical project depends on (or, less favorably, is stretched upon the procrustean bed of) the transcendental logic. What is the status of that logic, or, in other words, what kind of knowledge is that given by the *Critiques*?

I suppose Kant would say "critical," and mean by that his own complex combination of rationalism and empiricism, idealism and pragmatism. It is a kind of knowledge which exhibits the sources of its truth at the same time as it offers conviction (universal agreement of all rational beings) about that truth. What looks to be a completely rationalistic underpinning to the critical philosophy has, in Kant's own mind, an empirical model beneath, or at least, running parallel to it. The model is that of a scientific experiment.

As mentioned earlier, from first *Critique* to third Kant insists that his philosophy is an enquiry and an experiment (Axiv/Bxiv; B xxviiff, xixn), "not a doctrine"(*KRV*: "The Doctrine of Pure Reason;" *KU*: 176). This experiment is one in which the scientist's Reason "must not allow itself to be kept, as it were, in nature's leading strings, but must itself show the way with principles of judgement based on fixed laws, constraining nature to give answer to questions of Reason's own determining" (B xiii). With that last phrase we see Kant's other analogy for the critical project—that of the law court—tie in with the analogy of the scientific experiment. The fixed laws he chose to start from were the principles of judgement itself. These laws are the same for all judges; thus, when the only way to explain a difference in two kinds of judgement that all make is pushed to a distinction in those laws, that distinction must be the explanation. Since the principles of judgement are valid for all judging subjects and necessarily so (by the first *Critique*) the deduction-assumption of the third *Critique* justifies the principle of critical conviction. This principle is necessary for any scientific knowledge, for it, by linking our passive capacity with our active faculty, connects world to mind. It is also necessary for communication, since only because of its sameness in all do we have an intersubjective (i.e. objective) world at all. Since the preconceptual intersubjectivity which lies at the base of aesthetic judgements is the only ground for the possibility of knowledge, learning, and communication among human beings, it is clear that Kant is not doing faculty psychology, but giving a well-thought out, though complex and occasionally unclear, argument. A psychologist has only one of Kant's models guiding him: an experiment showing how things work in fact. Kant also is giving an argument about why things must work in accord with the principles of transcendental logic, not just that they do so work. It is the combination of the two models (or sets of two models: rationalist/empiricist, idealist/pragmatist, law court/experiment) that makes his philosophy critical, for each model sets boundaries to the employment of the other.[13] It strikes me as quite interesting that Kant, who seems to be the thoroughgoing defender of the rational, should, with critical conviction, exhibit shared feeling as what *must* be met with in experience, in comparison with moral actions which *could* be met with in experience, and knowledge of the empirical which *is* experienced (Cf. A807/B835). It makes one think that perhaps the modern concern with epistemology first is upside down (by its own greatest light). An ironist would, perhaps, make much of this; the romantics certainly did.

There is another way to look at the question of truth—and the truth of Kant's deductions—which provides a broader picture of what seems to be organizing the tropes of Kant's philosophy and underlying the deferrals we have been tracing. According to Northrop Frye there are "three organizations of myths and archetypal symbols in literature."[14] They may be called mythic, romantic, and realistic. There is a theory of truth which can be associated with each type of organization of symbols: Frye calls them mythic identification, coherence, and correspondence respectively. In the course of the critical project Kant uses all three theories, and in following the problem of hope we have seen how one theory of truth has displaced another as we have moved from one type of organization of symbols to another. The question of hope first arose in the theoretical philosophy; there the theory of truth is that of "realism"—correspondence of thought to object (Cf. A58/B83, A191/B236)—but since "the world" is never given as an object, the hope for a complete *Naturwissenschaft* was displaced to practical reason. In the realm of practical reason the question transformed itself from whether or not the world corresponds to our thought to whether or not a world connecting the ends of theory with the ends of practical reason could be coherent. Kant argued that such a combination is not incoherent and that for practical reason freedom is a fact. In order to argue in any positive fashion for the unity of the world, we must step back to the final level of symbolic organization: myth.[15] This Kant does in the third *Critique* where the ideal human moral world becomes identified with the world. Kant's words are that "the beautiful is the symbol of the moral." This identification of the "real" world with the world of reason—an identification which cannot be discovered by realism (since the whole is never given), and which is the possibility which drives romanticism, but which the romantic cannot prove—is mythic. Man is the measure of all things, of what is that it is, of what is not that it is not.

If a person were to say "the truth is subjectivity," one thing he might be pointing to by that statement (assuming every statement refers to something else which is the truth of its content) is that the more ordinary senses of truth—truth in the realistic sense of correspondence, truth in the romantic sense of coherence—are parasitic upon the mythic form of identification. Since judgement is the keystone of the architectonic, and since the principle of this faculty is subjectively universal, not universally subjective (objec-tive), it seems that Kant might be agreeing with such a position. Of course it doesn't seem that such a position can really be held since to say "the truth as correspondence is parasitic upon truth as identification" seems to refer to a state of affairs such that the statement is true if and only if reality is such that it corresponds to that statement, which makes the parasite into the host. Kant, assuming he would want to agree that "the truth is subjectivity," might reiterate his earlier points in order to answer this paradox:

1) "Reality" is not given to us as a whole in order to test that statement which seems to claim a correspondence.

2) Coherence has no claim to being a theory of *truth* unless it can find some way to be linked to "the world" (as freedom is).

3) "The beautiful is the symbol of the moral"—the coherent moral whole, the intelligible world, is "in" the phenomenal world. There is a symbolic identification of the two.

Mythopoeia is not subject to correspondence or coherence, but sets the limits for what is to count as "corresponding to" the world and allows coherence to "have a reference" and thus claim to be a theory of *truth*. Myth is the gin of truth: It tells you what to look for to bring to it, it turns out a certain kind of product that another gin won't. One could well ask "of all the gin joints in all the world, why did we walk in to this one?" I'm not sure if that kind of question ever gets answered. On a more philosophical note, if these remarks about "the truth is subjectivity" are "true," perhaps it explains why Socrates is always telling stories. When he explains to Meno that color is an effluence of the eye rebounding from the objects he prefaces that explanation by saying "here is a story which is something like what you are accustomed to." Meno buys it. At the end of *Republic* he tells a story which, if nothing else, provides a framework for a life in which one worries about what virtue is and how it is achieved. That myth explains why both the questions within the dialogue and dialogue itself are taken to heart. In fact, that myth demands both. Still more to the point about Kant, to say that the beautiful is the symbol of the moral is not just a mythic identification: intuited world = moral world, it is also a statement which claims correspondence—the world we intuit is a moral world; and a claim of coherence—the world of sense hangs together with the world of morality. If it is both of these, it is also open to a test, the same test every scientific claim is open to: go look. Is it not the case that an experience of the beautiful—say a perfect yellow rose, or Rilke's *Elegies*—activates all of your powers—intellectual, moral, feeling—in a pleasurable way? And isn't such a work or flower a whole world of which you are (for a moment?) a part? Here each of us must judge for herself. On the other hand, "the truth is subjectivity" does not mean the truth is whatever you think, because judgement is also an act of Reason.

3. Can the Proof be Reconstituted?

As a matter of course philosophers these days don't have much faith in myth. Can we reduce Kant's mythopoeia to philosophical categories? At the end of the argument for the principle of judgement Kant allowed the assumption of a rule for judgement which would link the active faculties of each to the passive capacity of each in the same way for all. The assumption is allowable because it is absolutely necessary for communication. And Kant is absolutely right about that. The whole critical experiment works insofar as it is an effort at answering the hyperbolic epistemological problem mentioned earlier. But the assumption of a rule for judgement which ties the critical experiment together and guarantees the possibility of communication creates the need for a distinction in the kinds of conviction. Since feeling is communicable there can now be two kinds of conviction: 1) a conviction grounded in communicable validity for all Reasonable beings (including God, angels, and Martians), 2) a conviction based in communicable validity for all humans—beings with our happy interplay of Reason and intuition. This second form is "subjectively universal validity"[16] and from it "no conclusion can be drawn to the logical [validity of the judgement] because judgements of [this] kind have no bearing upon the object" (*KU*: 215).

Now the judgement about the necessary connection of happiness with the moral end is obviously this second kind of judgement, for happiness is not an end of pure reason. Kant, of course, presents the union of virtue and happiness as an end any reasonable being (including God) must affirm, and its contrary as repugnant to reason. But can a purely rational being even have an idea of happiness, tied up as it is with inclination and intuition? Can God, who has no passions, have an idea of passion satisfied? It seems that such an idea—unsatisfied passion connected to a worthy will, or the satisfaction of the unworthy—can only be repugnant to a reason connected through intuition to inclination and feeling. Kant's own arguments seem to indicate as much, for in proving beneficence a duty he reasons that our own self-love cannot be divorced from our need of help from others, so we make ourselves an end for others. But the only way for making ourselves an end for others to cohere with a system of universal law is if we will to make other men our ends too (*DV*: 393). Now at least some of these needs of ours are needs touching upon our moral vocation—for example our need for education. The existence of such needs puts autonomy at risk and

makes the human moral community one of mutual inter-
independence. Such inter-independence, however, may not be the
case with all rational beings. It is certainly not the case between
human beings and God: It is impossible for a purely rational being,
a perfect being, to have an interest in happiness. Hence there is only
a subjectively universal validity to the judgement that patient merit
without happiness or unworthiness with happiness is "repugnant to
reason" (*FMM*: 394). Such a judgement is one about which "no
conclusion can be drawn" concerning logical validity. "The law
says only that I should sacrifice a part of my well-being to others
without hope of requital ... it cannot assign determinate limits to the
extent of this sacrifice" (*DV*: 393, my italics). Both our duty and our
needs have objective grounds, but the hope for a moral world order
where happiness accords with desert is not objective.

B. The (In)Ability of the Will

But there is room for judgement here. Judgement, to whose defect
"all errors of subreption are to be ascribed.... [n]ever to understanding or to reason" (A643/B671). Perhaps philosophy's way of
regarding things as true, philosophy's penchant for realism or
romanticism is just "a story something like what we are
accustomed to," so let us begin again by assuming Kant's critical
mythopoeia is true. It does, after all, have the advantage of
explaining how the realism of science and the romance of morality
can both be true at the same time, each in its own way. No small
feat. And both seem to be actual ongoing projects, so we need some
kind of explanation—if only to avoid following these lives
unexaminedly. So then, given that "it is only the moral relations of

men to men that are intelligible to us" and given that "the sort of
moral relation that holds between God and man surpasses
completely the boundaries of [philosophy] and is altogether inconceivable to us" (*DV*: 490), is it reasonable for us just as *men to
men* to hope for a moral world order? Let us for a moment speak
man to man with a character who seems to have judged Kant's
critical project with a fair eye and affirmed it.

One of the few catholic doctrines among Kierkegaard's
interpreters is that the second volume of *Either/Or* and the character
of Judge Wilhelm owes much to Kant. The Judge seems to be just the
person Kant's *Foundations* is addressed to. He would willingly
follow whither it would lead him: From his "ordinary rational
knowledge of morality to the philosophical," "from popular moral
philosophy to a metaphysics of morals," and "from a metaphysics of
morals to a critique of practical reason."[17]   Further, all our
instruments agree that the moral project of the Judge is shown up by
the "Ultimatum" of *Either/Or* to be impossible. The Judge is
therefore in despair.

Judge Wilhelm should have recognized this himself. He writes,
in a letter to his aesthetic friend:

> *But he who says that he wants to enjoy life always
> posits a condition which either lies outside the
> individual or is in the individual in such a way that
> it is not posited by the individual himself.* With
> respect to this last sentence I would beg you to hold
> fast the expressions I have used, for they are chosen
> deliberately (*E/Or*: II, 184).

The sentence he begs us not to change is emphasized by his own hand—he knows it is of critical importance in his long-winded letter. But what is he afraid the aesthete might change within it? An aesthete with a philosophical bent might drop out the phrase "to enjoy life." Does the truth value of the sentence which we are begged not to change change?

> *He who says that he wants* always posits a condition which either lies outside the individual or is in the individual in such a way that it is not posited by the individual himself.

That, too, seems true. And if we add "to achieve a moral world order in which happiness accords with desert" in place of "to enjoy life"? Clearly, as Kant admits, this posits a couple of conditions—God, another life—conditions which lie outside himself. But what if we substitute this other and purely rational end, "to become worthy?" There is food for thought here:

> *He who says that he wants to become worthy always posits a condition which either lies outside the individual or is in the individual in such a way that it is not posited by the individual himself.*

A few pages later, after giving an outline of the stages of aestheticism—a developmental analysis of the person who "wants to enjoy life" which exhibits that the backside of this life is melancholy—the Judge concludes:

> Let each learn what he can, at least we both can learn that a man's unhappiness is never due to the fact that

he has not the outward conditions in his power, this
being the very thing which would make him unhappy
(193).

Very well.   The common rational knowledge of morality
understands that

> even if it should happen that, by a particularly
> unfortunate fate or by the niggardly provision of a
> step-motherly nature, the will should be wholly
> lacking in power to accomplish its purpose, ... it
> would sparkle like a jewel [for which] usefulness or
> fruitfulness ... could only be its setting (*FMM*: 394).

But what about what "lies in the individual?" If becoming worthy
posits a condition which is outside of the individual's power, then the
moral life is—from its commanded beginning to its hoped for end—
unhappy. We speak here not of outward conditions, but of the
inward condition.

In the early moral writings Kant seems just to assume that since
there is a categorical imperative, we must be able to fulfill it. This
"must implies can" doctrine is unexamined until the *Religion*. In
that book Kant examines the possibility of the "indwelling of
radical evil in human nature." If "the subjective ground of the
exercise of man's freedom in general" (*Rel*: 16) is radically and
ineradicably evil, then it would seem that the doctrine that must
implies can is a lie. What we must do is produce a good will in
ourselves; if evil is radically and ineradicably present we cannot.
Fulfilling the moral law is an impossibility. A sublime and noble

impossibility perhaps, but impossible nonetheless. "Taint not your mind against your mother aught...."

The major point of the *Critique of Practical Reason* can be refined after the *Religion* as an "analysis of *Wille*" and that of the *Foundations* as an "analysis of *Willkür*," the power of choice. *Willkür* can choose to be determined by *Wille* or not.[18] In the former case *Willkür* is good, in the latter it is "a real and contrary determination of the *Willkür*, i.e., an opposition to the law, i.e., an evil *Willkür*." With regard to one's moral disposition it is either/ or: "there is no middle ground" (18n). One's moral disposition is an act of *Willkür*, the subjective ground of which act we "cannot know" and which disposition we cannot derive "from any original act of the *Willkür* in time" (20, 21). So our moral disposition has the following qualities according to Kant: First, it is an act of free choice, that is, this disposition is imputable to us—we are its parents and originals. Second, we not only cannot be sure of the morality of our maxims—as the *Foundations* pointed out—but we cannot know the ground or the worth of our moral disposition (which is the explanatory ground for holding some maxims and rejecting others). Third, this disposition, grounded as it is in transcendental freedom, is not chosen by any original act in time, but is the ground on which all other choices of maxims in time are made. Our moral disposition could be called our "Maxim of maxims."

Kant's analysis of our disposition makes clear that there is an "indwelling of the evil principle with the good" in our nature, that both are radical and ineradicable. This indwelling of both principles is due to the fact that *Wille* and *Willkür* are not the same thing for us (for God they are). Our power of choice (*Willkür*) can be

determined by pure reason (*Wille*) or it can choose another
determining ground. It (*Willkür*) can also be determined by sensible considerations. However, that it can be so determined does not
imply that sense is evil. The evil is in the *Willkür* which strays
from its own internal legislator (*Wille*). On the contrary, our
sensuous nature is as equally the ground of the possibility of virtue
as it is of vice (30).

Our propensity to evil is a "predisposition to crave a delight
which, when once experienced, arouses an inclination" (24n). This
seems to indicate that our predisposition to the good is *a priori*, while
our propensity to evil is *a posteriori*, but Kant describes the
propensity to evil as always already present: it is "a subjective
determining ground of the *Willkür* which precedes all acts and
which, therefore, is ... an act [adopting a supreme maxim] in the first
sense (*peccatum originarium*)" (26). But if "predisposition" is what
is "original,"[19] then the distinction propensity/predisposition
evaporates for we have originally experienced the delight of
disobedience to *Wille's* law subjecting happiness to worthiness.
The inclination is already aroused, *Willkür* is always already
divided, impure, lacking singlemindedness and integrity (24-25).
Tainted.

Our predisposition to the good is more easily explained. It is
simply the presence of *Wille* as an incentive of *Willkür*. Clearly
these predispositions (to good and evil) are grounded in *Willkür* not
in *Wille* and sensible desire respectively. And each is as radical
and ineradicable as the other. But then having a good will is either
trivial, since *Wille* is always so, or impossible, since *Willkür* is
always (in us) divided. The best we can hope for is that the battle

within *Willkür* will, with regard to the maxims we act upon in time, always be in accord with *Wille*. But Kant insists on the stronger point that "for man ... who despite a corrupted heart yet possesses a good *Wille* there remains hope of a return to the good from which he has strayed" (39). What makes this hope possible?

In a general observation concerning this restoration Kant becomes oxymoronic, paradoxical, self-contradictory. The reader is left to decide upon his own interpretation.

> Granted that some supernatural cooperation may be
> necessary to his becoming good, ... a man must first
> make himself worthy to receive it, and must lay hold
> of this aid (which is no small wonder).

No small wonder indeed, since worthiness is already defined as having a good will.

> Despite the fall, the injunction that we ought to
> become better men resounds unabatedly in our souls;
> hence this must be within our power, even though
> what we are able to do is itself inadequate (40).

But if we are inadequate, then it is clearly not within our power. There is a condition which either lies outside the individual or lies within him in such a way that it is not posited by himself. Kant tries one more time to place the required condition within the individual and within the individual's power. One more attempted answer.

C. The (Non)Temporality of Eternal Striving

And one more deferral. The restoration we hope for is "not the acquiring of a lost incentive for the good"—man is unthinkable without *Wille*, which provides that incentive. The "restoration is but the establishment of the purity of this law as the supreme ground of all our maxims," (42) as the Maxim of maxims. There are two ways to think this restoration: *either* reformation, *or* revolution.

By adopting maxims which accord with duty, a man, with each successive adoption takes a step on "the road of endless progress to holiness" (42) or virtue. As Aristotle pointed out, becoming virtuous begins in that way—by performing actions in accord with virtue, but in order to have true virtue the actions need not only to be in accord with virtue, but also done as the virtuous man would do them and from a firm and stable character. Kant requires that the maxims of one's action not only accord with duty, but also that the incentive be duty. Our complete restoration would be to have the Maxim of our maxims be firm and stable. Kant is well aware that practicing virtue—repeatedly choosing actions which are in accord with duty, is no guarantee that one is practicing actions whose incentive is duty, though the practice of virtue will lead to a tendency to have maxims that are in accord with it. The Reformation can lead only to a change of practices, can make one legally good, but moral goodness—a change of heart—requires a revolution. Since the moral disposition of *Willkür* is non-temporal, no temporal practices can touch it.

A revolution in *Willkür* would be rooting out (44) the evil predisposition. But as this predisposition is original and non-temporal, so the rooting out must be non-temporal. And original.

Aye, there's the rub, for as soon as there are two acts, there is time, there is before and after. "For were there ... change, ... there would also be time, since change can occur only in time, and without the presupposition of time nothing can be thought of" (End: 334). Let us speak man to man:

Does not this restoration through one's own exertions directly contradict the postulate of the innate corruption of man (*Rel*: 46)?

"Yes, to be sure, so far as the conceivability, i.e., our *insight* into the possibility, of such restoration is concerned" (46).

This is true of everything which is to be regarded as an event in time (as change), and to that extent as necessary under the laws of nature, while at the same time its opposite is to be represented as possible through freedom under moral laws (46).

"Yet the postulate in question is not opposed to the possibility of this restoration itself" (46).

But now we have arrived at a kind of inconceivability which is significantly different from the earlier inconceivability of how it may be the case that the world is a world in which happiness accords with deserts. Now we have this kind of inconceivability: two original and opposing acts by the same being. Now we have contradiction.[20]

"[But] when the moral law commands that we ought now to be better men, it follows inevitably that we must be able to be better men" (46).[21]

But what of this circumstance of innate and original corruption?
It is given, then how should I begin?[22]

"We must begin with the incessant counteraction against [the
inextirpable propensity to evil]" (46).

But it is far too late to begin at that beginning and it is impossible
for this work to achieve its end!

"Yet he must be able to hope through his own efforts to reach the
road which leads thither" (46).

Why?

"Because he ought to become a good man and is to be adjudged
morally good only by virtue of that which can be imputed to him as
performed by himself" (46).

But we have already seen that this is not merely an
inconceivable *how*, but an inconceivable *that*, i.e., a contradiction.
It looks like Reason is deceiving us. She is running away! Quick,
is there some other virtue which could be imputed to us?

"We can admit a work of grace as something
incomprehensible, but we cannot adopt it into...the maxims of
reason, if she is to remain within her limits" (48-49).

> *"Naar det andagtsfulde Sind finder Alt for-*
> *fængeligt, saa gjør det ingen Undtagelse med sin*

egen Person, gjør ingen Ophævelser med den,
tvertimod, den maa ogsaa tilside, for at det
Guddommelige ikke skal stødes tilbage ved dens
Modstand" (SV, XIII, 332).

Oh no. I'm afraid she has gone away.

Create in me a new heart, O God,
And renew a steadfast spirit within me.
Cast me not out—"

Concluding Symbolic Postscript

to

the Man to Man Conversation

So then, the moral project as outlined by Kant is impossibly
unreasonable. Well, then we just give it up. Why? Because it is
impossible. How eminently rational(?) ... practical(?) ... well, ...
pragmatic anyway. Would that things were so simple. They are
not. Kant argues that "reason can be satisfied with nothing save an
end of its own making" (*FMM*: 396), in which case it is against
reason to give up the moral end. It is intrinsic to a being with a
Wille. Human praxis is defined by the possibility of morality, it is
impossible to give the moral end up without ceasing to be human.[23]
Earlier in this chapter Kant's moral theory was compared with that
form of symbolic organization called romance in Frye's sense.
Now we can see that his theory has an element of the more common
understanding of romanticism in it. In fact the romantic could be a
"symbol of" the moral man here: Suppose one is in love with a

woman; she marries. Does the romantic trade in his love for her
and take up with the butcher's daughter—who is quite as good a
match? No. Then he would cease to be the romantic. Does he then
attempt to break the marriage, tempt her from her vows? That is
unthinkable, how could a lover desire to commit adultery with the
one he loves, or think it a real possibility for the beloved? To do so
would be to cease being the lover.

The cure is to die—to "die from." A desperate hope. *Fiat
voluntas tua ...*

Chapter 3:

THE CHARACTER OF THE RELIGIOUS IN KIERKEGAARD'S DRAMA

I: A Pathetic Mimic Deduction and an Edifying Possibility

> Literature shapes itself, and is not shaped externally.
>
> ——Northrop Frye

In order to continue this project I need a clear "point of view." Kant was obviously a philosopher. The philosophical point of view was clearly appropriate. What is Kierkegaard's authorship?

What is any authorship?[1]

Here is a possibility for edification. An authorship is like a self in Anti-Climacus' understanding: "A relation which relates itself to its own self [which relation] ... must either have constituted itself or have been constituted by another" (*SUD*: 146). What is the significance of this Hegelian pseudo-psychology?

Take for example a rose, which by any other word would smell as sweet. It has its parts—petals, sepal, stem, roots, thorns—related to each other. They are related to each other quite naturally, and since this relation is unreflectively accomplished, it makes sense to say the parts are related rather than that they relate themselves to each other. A ship, on the other hand, has parts that are related to each other by reflection—not by its own reflection of course—but unlike the rose, the ship does not become a ship of its own accord, rather only with the help of and by means of the decisions of its designers and builders. In fact, unlike the rose, the ship has nothing to do with its own making. A self, on the other hand, becomes what it is by its own reflection and choices and work upon what it has as its "parts:" its history, its talents, its place in the world, its possibilities, its necessities.

The authorship of Søren Å. Kierkegaard is clearly not like a rose. Unless, of course, you want to buy the romantic notion that the author is merely the pen-holder for the spirit, and the force that through the green fuse drives the flower drives his black ink—and with as little reflection. That actually sounds rather nice, but it is, most probably, only a very pretty lie. To continue in the same mood: An authorship is also not like a simple lute, placed lengthwise in the clasping casement of its covers, by the desultory wind carressed— more like some coy maid half yielding to her lover...

But, forward: What is wrong with both romantic notions is that they make the individual authorship disappear. It is evaporated into the force, or is a mere instrument for any wind that blows. Clearly though, an authorship has an element of personal style which the force lacks, and on the other side, authorships resist some interpretations; not every reader can make one sing. That is from the point of view of a reader or critic. From the point of view of this writer—on re-reading—it is obvious that I am winding a tedious argument of some intent through these pages. Before the face of these two points of view (reader-critic and writer-reader) the romantic notion of authorship retreats.

Many readers of the corpus of an author read with the seemingly scientifically accurate point of view that the body of the text does not move, but the reader's eye moves over it. Where there is no motion there is no life, hence an authorship, like any human artifact, is a collection of parts reflectively related and put together by the reflection and decision of other parties, in this case readers. Among those readers, one is credited with being the author, and it is by analogy to his work that the other readers are said to have read/understood his book. The reader imitates the authorized mental movements (whether conscious or unconscious) and in so doing gets the point. Get the point? But if you do get the point, then how can there be disagreements among artificiandos of an authorship such as "what kind of 'ship is it?" and "can it float?" And how can it be that when you come back to the same authorship you can identify it differently—how can it be that you hear it differently (as exhibited in the proem's soundings of Kierkegaard's authorship where at least three quite different songs were heard)? Have we gone back to the same 'ship? Are you sure?

That a text is a human artifact—that it is constituted by another—does not mean it is more like a ship than a self. According to Anti-Climacus, a self is a relation which relates itself to itself and in so doing is related to another who constituted it. Things could then be summarized this way: authorships only exist for readers—no authorship, no reader, and the converse: no reader, no authorship. This is clearly different from the ordinary under-standing of both ship and rose, for the one may well be afloat without sailors or any presently existing builders and the other may dwell among the untrodden ways. An authorship, on the other hand, in order to relate itself to itself needs a presently existing reader constituting it.

"But," an impatient interlocutor objects, "is an authorship

really different from another artifact, like a ship? An authorship does not construct itself reflectively, the reader reflectively constructs, constitutes the relation between the parts of the 'ship." This seems to be slipping back into the "merely empirical" scientistic view that all the materials are there and we just construct and sail it. However, as someone like Kant would say, this "assembling of materials in a merely technical manner" is no explanation for the conditions of the possibility of the assembly (A834/B862). The classical explanation of an authorship—that the author builds and each reader sails—assumes that the 'ship is there, whether the reader is or not. The next plausible explanation—that the reader constructs the 'ship on the plan of the author—loses its polish when one asks questions about the conditions for the possibility of either 1) knowing the author's plan for his 'ship, or 2) words having any significance within a text at all.[2] If we are to be able at all to put an authorship together in the way the purely empirical reader thinks we do, then there must be an "affinity of the manifold" (A113f) parts of the authorship—the words as well as the works. In that case the question "what is any authorship?" becomes what is the nature of this affinity? If we say it is a transcendental affinity we are saying that "it is nowhere to be found save in the principle of the unity" (A122) of the authorship. But this affinity is one of the very conditions for the unity of the authorship, so such an answer doesn't help much.

This mock transcendental question has an empirical problem associated with it, for it seems clear to every reader of a text that there are relations between the parts: echoes, analogical style shifts between parts, plays on and with the words, and that these relations are there, not imagined to be there by some absolutely free subjectivity. And it seems this way to every reader, even the original reader called the author. An author is often surprised by "his own" texts. That texts can read this way even to an author indicates that an authorship is not a thing built simply from a blueprint of intentions. It seems that this empirical fact is one reason poets have a tendency to answer questions of the form "did you mean x in poem y?" with "Lady, if I had wanted to mean x I would have said x!"

To explore what the affinity of the manifold of an authorship could be like let us return to our three analogies. The affinity which is the condition for the possibility of an authorship could be a) like a rose, b) like a ship, or c) like a self. That is, the affinity of texts in an authorship (or words in a text) which affinity is the condition for the possibility of the authorship (or a text) can be a) natural and unreflective, b) non-natural and reflective, c) natural and reflective. That the affinity of words and texts in an authorship is only poetically like a rose has already been defended. That the affinity of texts in an authorship is like that of a ship is no more an explanation for their unity than the transcendental maneuver was.[3] But to say that the affinity of the manifold which is the condition for the possibility of an authorship is like a self seems helpful. It seems true: language looks like the natural structure of reflection. It is also edifying.

A self is a relation which relates itself to itself and does so either by constituting itself, or by relating itself to another which constitutes it. If the latter, then it is precisely in relating itself to itself that it relates itself to the power which constitutes it. This is

exactly how things are with an authorship. It is a relation between
the phonemes, words, concepts, works; the text itself is a relation of
necessity and possibility as structuralism has shown. The reader
constitutes the authorship as a relation; the authorship is a relation
insofar as it is constituted to be so by the reader. Whether an authorship exists without readers is a question which forgets the founding
definition of this view of reading: Authorship and reader are
correlative terms. A non-reader cannot ask about an authorship, as
soon as he does he is *ipso facto* a reader. The derived, constituted
relation which is an authorship relates itself to itself only by being
constituted by another (the reader). Such a derived, constituted
relation is completely dependent for its being. But since an
authorship is constituted as a relation which relates itself to itself the
reader himself is not totally independent with regard to it.

This seems to make the author no more authoritative than the
reader. If that is the case, it at least agrees with one of the
confessions made by S. Kierkegaard (under his own name) about
his authorship:

> My relation is even more external than that of a poet,
> who poetizes characters, and yet in the preface is
> himself the author. For I am impersonal, or am
> impersonal in the second person, a *souffluer* who has
> poetically produced the authors, whose preface in
> turn is their own production, as are even their own
> names. So in the pseudonymous works there is not a
> single word which is mine, I have no opinion about
> these works except as a third person, no knowledge of
> their meaning except as a reader, not the remotest

private relation to them, since such a thing is impossible" ("First and Last Declaration," in *CUPS*: 551).

That the analogy of text to self provides a foundation for understanding Kierkegaard's practice of writing and his own understanding of his works is authority enough for me to accept the analogy.

But I would also have this edifying view of reading speak to you, *kære læser*. Perhaps a theological analogy will make the point clearer: An authorship is to a reader almost as a human self is to its Originator. The first party in each half of the analogy ('ship or self) is a relation. Each is a derived, constituted relation (constituted by the power which is the other half of each side of the analogy: reader or God). The derived relation may be understood in each case as a relation of necessity and possibility, finitude and infinitude, consciousness and unconsciousness (Freudian critics read both texts and selves this way). Note that none of these—should I call them structural?—modes of interpretation of either the 'ship or self require reference to the "original" constituting power—an author instituting his intention, or a God. On the other hand, one can also easily see how, according to this analogy, a person would be led to think that there *is* such a constituting power. In that case the text or self is most clearly and truly understood when it is understood in proper relation to the power which constitutes it. If the Originator of the text or self were of infinite power (symbolized by an ability to create *ex nihilo*), it would be possible for the creation to be one of infinite jest and freedom. If the Originator is less powerful (symbolized by fashioning out of an already existent material), the creation would be neither completely free nor completely under the originator's control, since the pre-existent material is a principle of counter-finality within the work. The theological analogy casts a (more or less) giant shadow: the relation text/reader implies a third—the author—who constitutes both the possibility of the text/reader relationship and its first actuality, since author is reader.

It is no longer fashionable to attempt to understand one's human self by reference to God. It seems completely possible to do without such a transcendent hypothesis. The old-fashioned story has an explanation even for the possibility of doing without its Prime Hypothesis: the author-God created a being of complete independence. Human author-readers are not completely free: An authorship is inextricably involved with both author and reader, for it does not exist without both. But this is a double bind, for both author and reader are, as well, incompletely independent from an authorship. S. Kierkegaard could have chosen never to write, but once he did he was no longer completely free. And you, *kære læser*, could have chosen not to read this, but now.... Alas, you see how it is. Only if an authorship is a combination of active and passive powers—like a self—can reading be, as it is, both an active (forming) and a passive (being formed) operation. And only under those same conditions can writing be both creative and iterative, repressive and freeing. To bind, and to loose, that means to write.

The interdependence of dependent text and incompletely independent reader is an essentially edifying view of reading. An authorship, indeed, cannot be thought to exist without a reader, but on the other side, the reader's possibilities in relation to any particular authorship are limited by the way the authorship relates itself to itself and in doing so relates itself to the reader who constitutes it. Thus the relation (authorship/reader) is very much like that of a human being in society. A human being is dependent upon society—one only becomes human within it—but society is incompletely independent of each human being within it. Just as society cannot (and should not attempt to) transform a human being into whatever it pleases, so too a reader cannot, for example, say that either SÅK's authorship or this little piece is a tale stolen from 1001 Nights about fish-mongering in 16th century Chicago. To say so would indicate that the reader was a reader of something else, but not of Kierkegaard's authorship. Two principles follow for (literary) aesthetics: There neither is, nor can be, nor ought an artist try to make a "free"—in the sense of hermetically shut up in itself, purely centripetal, non-centrifugal—"autonomous verbal structure."[4] It may also be the case that this literary principle extends throughout aesthetics. I, at any rate, would not be surprised if that were the case. Kant might be. Secondly, the reader's task and play are qualitatively the same as the author's: each exists in relation to the text as the constituting power of the text. This is why the best writers can make us better readers. Reading and criticism, not only poetry and drama, are works of art.

It follows then, that there are many ways in which an authorship may exist. Kant's authorship clearly relates itself to itself as a philosophical one: the way it relates itself to itself permits no other way of constituting it; it requires its reader to take it that way. "Require" here has the force of a moral command: if you would treat the authorship as it would be treated, or if you would make the

ends of the authorship your own ends insofar as that is possible.[5]
This requirement is edifying: it builds up—encourages—the
practice of morality in a reader. Some readers, like some people,
refuse to treat other selves as ends in themselves and so there result
perverse readings of authorships (just as there exist perverse
relationships between persons), and such perversions can be
performed even upon authorships as autonomous as Kant's. SÅK's
authorship does not request a specific constitution *uno voce*, the
voices are, rather, legion. The critic then, who—to speak strictly—
stands as a mediator between an authorship and a reader (the latter
could be called the reader at second hand), is in a difficult spot here.
A morally difficult spot if the analogy of the text to a self is taken
with all its edifying force. To represent Kierkegaard's authorship
in a way which allows each reader to constitute it in his or her own
way is preferable to representing the authorship as a "philosophical"
or "theological" or "seductive-aesthetic" one. I would not be a
fascistic critic who bends an authorship to remove it to his own will
and purposes. Oh, no. It is within the power of any other reader to
attempt to do so. As with some people, some authorships are more
easily bent to dictatorial purposes. In my opinion the principle of
charity is preferable in both the case of persons and authorships.
Such a principle allows the hope of each person, and each reader, to
lie in his own conscience.[6]

   This essentially ethical view of reading is one I have followed
from the beginning. Reading is a type, a synecdochic type to be
exact, of ethics. In order to accomplish the purpose of leaving the
authorship as free as possible, let us say that all the names—Søren
Å. Kierkegaard, S. Kierkegaard, Johannes de Silentio, *et al.*—are
the names of characters in a drama.[7] Whether the drama is closer

in theme and purpose to a medieval mystery play or to a famous opera by Mozart I leave up to the conscience of the fair reader. Within this drama of the authorship there are insets: plays within the play, which have a double function.   1) They further the development of the drama which is the authorship.   2) They allow a clear presentation of one or another aspects of one or more characters who appear in a more completely dialectical fashion in the "real life" of the larger drama.[8] The inset play also presents some of the motives at work in the other characters, but in the real life of the drama the motives of the inset are not the full explanation.[9] My critical inquiry will not center on plot, the unity of time or place (or lack of it), or $\mu\epsilon\lambda o\sigma$ and diction, but on character in the drama of Kierkegaard's authorship.

II: The Theological Virtues in Several Characters

> Sailing heart-ships through broken harbors, out on
> the waves in the night ...
>
> ——*Tell Me Why*, Neil Young

Within a drama every character "must necessarily in all instances represent things in one or another of three ways: either as they were or are, or as they are said or thought to be or have been, or as they ought to be," *således skal det være efter Æsthetikens Regler* laid down by Aristotle (*Poetics* 1460b9-11). As a matter of fact, all three ways are represented in Kierkegaard's authorship. His poetic project is nothing if not complete. But there is more than a mere passion for completeness here, for the best way to present a certain

type of character is to present him from several points of view in
several situations. This is exactly what the drama does: the
characters themselves are something, they interact with other
characters who are something else, they comment from their own
points of view upon the other characters—some of whom are like
themselves, others different—and the beliefs, artistry, love affairs
and self-consciousness (or lack thereof) of those other characters,
and, as in Plato's dialogues, no one character has or gives the full
picture, that is, no one character controls the play. (Though S.
Kierkegaard makes the strongest bid for such control—after the
death of SÅK.) There is no guarantee that any one character is the
ventriloquist's dummy for the author. It is possible that Kierkegaard's presentation of the religious is for the purpose of edifying
readers, as the religious characters would have it. The larger
drama is then like a mystery play. It is equally possible that the
presentation is one which outdoes *Don Giovanni*, for by far the best
way to insure the success of the secondary seduction (i.e., the
seduction of the world) is to present the specifically religious
characters (who go under the names Anti-Climacus and S.
Kierkegaard, *blandt andet*) in an accurate fashion. As one of the
religious characters says: "deception extends equally as far as
love" (*WL: passim*).

Since only the ideal (what ought to be) is unified (the actual and
the thought to be are, as Aristotle indicates, broken instantly by time
into the past and present), it is only by comparison with the unified
ideal that the real becomes understandable. It makes sense to begin,
then, by investigating what Kierkegaard presents as Christianity
"as it ought to be." In his *Journals* SÅK leads us to believe that
Christianity as it ought to be is represented primarily in Anti-

Climacus' works, i.e., *The Sickness Unto Death* and *Training in Christianity*. These two works are edited by the self-avowedly religious writer, S. Kierkegaard, who, it seems, on his own part represents what Christianity is (thus is a step below the ideal, as actuality always is, in one sense, a fall from ideality) and who also seems to know, as does Anti-Climacus, what Christianity is thought to be (which is yet another step below ideality). Indeed, a careful reading of S. Kierkegaard's "Preface" to *Training in Christianity* will find mention of just those three representations of Christianity for which Aristotle's *Poetics* allows.[10] That S. Kierkegaard in his role as a religious writer publishes *Edifying Discourses* is a further indication of that character's liminal position between what Christianity is thought to be and what it ought to be for two reasons. First, facing what Christianity is thought to be, a discourse can only be edifying if it both reaches a reader where she is and can motivate her to move higher. Secondly, facing what Christianity ought to be, S. Kierkegaard does not publish discourses (*Taler*) "for edification," for such implies an author/ity (*Hjemmels/mand*) with which he is not at home.[11] He does, however, publish edifying discourses: discourses by which he—one who is not what he ought to be—is edified, and so discourses which he has reason to think will be edifying to others who are in a similar position.

Kierkegaard prided himself on being a great dialectician, and clearly he was justified in considering himself to be so.[12] His works are, as he himself, "dialectical through and through," and in fact, if one quality unites all of his writing from *The Concept of Irony* to the posthumous *Øjeblikket 10*, it is that.[13] The Christian discourses signed by S. Kierkegaard and the diagnostic, prognostic and prophylactic works of Anti-Climacus are no exceptions.

Because of this thorough-going dialecticality, once on the path which is outlined as a thought experiment by Johannes Climacus—the path which begins by affirming X, that there is something other than reason which is necessary—one gets everywhere else on the path eventually. So with regard to the theological virtues, starting with any one, one will arrive at the other two. "Starting" and "arriving" are merely logical terms, for it is with the theological virtues as Aristotle says it is with the moral virtues: if a person has one, he has all the others as well. The only problem then is to begin. And we begin with the ideal:

Faith

Anti-Climacus opposes faith to sin, despair, and offence. Let us begin with the last: "So inseparable from faith is the possibility of offence that if the God-Man were not the possibility of offence, He could not be the object of faith" (*TC*: 143). To put things in the algebraic form with which we began, the argument seems to be this: If something besides reason is necessary, this extra-rational something must reveal itself, but what is extra-rational is either the absurd or the seemingly absurd. If the latter, then that which needs to be revealed is ... rational. This contradicts the assumption that something besides reason is necessary.[14] Thus the extra-rational X must reveal itself to rational beings as the absurd. It cannot do otherwise if the answer to the first question is to be affirmative. If we call X the God-Man, then it is clear that the only way to believe in the God-Man is to believe the God-Man.[15]

But further, if X is truly outside of reason, and X can only make itself an object for faith, it cannot be made an object by reason, for in that case reason would have discovered very well that it needs something and X could only reveal that it exists. Moreover it would then be reason which shows that *this* X is what was necessary. But then the revelation would not be that something outside of reason is necessary, but rather that X exists, and if, as the argument above showed, X must reveal itself as the absurd, then reason would have shown that the absurd is necessary and the absurd would have revealed that it exists. This is not simply stupid, it is doubly so. Reason cannot show the absurd to be necessary and it is (even more?) impossible for the absurd to come into a real relation to reason. As Aristotle says, a contradiction can neither be nor be thought. From this, two conclusions follow: to believe X requires a completely and qualitatively different organ than reason. That organ is faith. Faith believes where reason is doubly offended. Secondly, in order to believe in God (where God is that X), one must believe God, not reason, for reason not only cannot believe, but it condemns as stupid and doubly stupid that X which is implied by an affirmative answer to our original question. Reason can, however, see this much: if (*per impossible*) there is an X, it is inseparable from offence. Where did this "if" come from? Parmenides, Aristotle, *et al.*, would say that a person who suggested such a thing had uttered words, but had not spoken. Every reasonable person agrees.

Both Climacus and Anti-Climacus clearly oppose faith to offence; they also agree on the opposition faith/sin. J.C. defines sin as the state of being in Error through one's own fault. Faith, on the other hand, is the condition given by the Unknown which remakes the learner in the truth. Let us go back to the original point of decision. One can answer the question whether besides reason anything else is necessary either affirmatively or negatively. If one answers negatively, but X is in fact necessary, one is in error, and by one's own choice—the negative answer. If in fact nothing else is necessary, then one is not in error. On the other hand, if one affirms that besides reason something else is necessary and in fact it is, she can only do so by faith, as was shown above. The fourth option J.C. thinks is impossible. It cannot be the case that one can answer the question "is X necessary" affirmatively and it be the case that X is not necessary. J.C. thinks that this conjunction is impossible because he reason cannot ask a question about whether or not X is necessary unless X (something else besides Reason which is necessary) has revealed itself. It is absurd to ask a question about the absurd. It cannot be a question. In the above paragraph it was noted that Aristotle, among others, would agree. If he is correct and the question can only be raised after that something necessary has appeared, then there are really only two, not three, alternatives: affirming (faith) or denying (sin) the reality of X. It is no longer possible to deny X and not be in error.[16]

J.C.'s argument that one cannot ask the question about X unless X has revealed itself would seem to prove that in fact X is necessary, since we have asked the question and the question can only be asked if X has appeared. This "proof" is absurd. Asking a question does not imply that an affirmative answer is the true one. Asking a question does not imply anything. That this "proof" is absurd is, according to J.C., neither unexpected nor any argument against it, given what we have already seen about the relationships obtaining between faith, thought and offence. That the proof is absurd is an obvious enough indication that it is not a proof.

Anti-Climacus presents his opposition between sin and faith a little more seriously than J.C., though he agrees that it is Christianity which first introduces consciousness of sin into the world, and that it would be "a dangerous objection against Christianity if paganism had a definition of sin which Christianity must admit is correct" (*SUD*: 220). But of course paganism cannot have this because sin is consciousness of existing before God and "with the conception of God to be in despair at not willing to be oneself" (*SUD*: 208). The requirement that sin be consciousness of existing before God demands that the Unknown has already revealed itself and that the Unknown needs to reveal itself indicates that human beings are already turned the wrong way (in sin). Therefore faith, the organ of appropriation, must be granted along with the revelation, and without it there is sin. If the first set of distinctions showed that faith is to *believe* God (and to believe anything else is to be offended, i.e. is not to believe, not to have faith at all), this set shows that faith *believes in* God, before whom one exists (and not to believe in God is to be in sin).

The final opposition which Anti-Climacus utilizes throughout the *Sickness* is despair/faith: "Christianity [the affirmative answer to our original question] has discovered an evil which man as such knows not of" (*SUD*: 145); this evil is despair. But Christianity also presents itself as the cure. A person may be willing to answer the first question affirmatively; that is, she may be able to overcome the offence. She may be able to admit further that she has been in sin. But she might then not be able to believe that her sin is forgiven. This is the highest form of despair; it is a refusal to believe that God has already done so. But this refusal indicates that one has really not got faith, for faith and sin are directly opposed, and the despairing one is still holding on to her sin. This form of despair is "closest to the religious" in the sense that it seems that offence has been avoided and sin recognized, which can only occur with faith. It is, however, also farthest away from the religious because while such a person is most conscious of existing before God, she will not ground herself in that Power, but holds with the energy of despair to herself: "No, I will not accept it: I have made myself this way and I will pay the just penalty." But this—in spite of the consciousness of God, in spite of the consciousness that before God one has been in error through one's own fault, and in spite of the fact that none of this is possible unless X has revealed itself—this is not faith, for faith is "by relating itself to its own self and by willing to be itself, to be grounded transparently in the Power which constituted it" (*SUD*: 262, *inter alia*). The last element of faith is *believing that* God has forgiven one's sins, commands the possible, is the power which constitutes one's self: not to accept this is the final effort against faith, it is defiance.

Two objections can be raised about the virtue of faith in Kierkegaard. They both have to do with its seeming intellectualism. First, why does his description of what is outside reason—the "X" affirmed at the start of his path—come in terms of contradiction and absurdity, why not the formless (as in early Greek philosophy—*apeiron*) or the monstrous (as in late Irish poetry—rough beast)? Second, why—granted the appearance of X is contradiction and absurdity—does Johannes Climacus, and following him Gene Fendt, present what can be the case after that fact in such a logical, foursquare manner?

One plausible answer to the first question is that Kierkegaard could be using the words "contradiction," "paradox," "absurd" on account of the dialectical necessities of his world-historical moment. S. Kierkegaard, the religious writer, complains about the philosyphication of Christianity in his day. Nothing could more surely end such blasphemy than by seeing Christianity as unmediatable contradiction. Whatever it is that faith is in such a case, it is not an adjunct to reason. In response to the second objection, that if the law of contradiction is violated by X there is no need to hold to the law in lining out the possibilities remaining after X has revealed itself I respond that a distinction should be made here: If, *per impossible*, X reveals itself, it is *X* which violates reason, but here reason is trying to outline possibilities and for reason to suggest violating the law of contradiction is for *reason* to violate itself and go over to the enemy. If there are to be contradictions it had better not be reason which begets them. Hence the logic of the argument should be followed. After X reveals itself the choices are more constrained: *either* faith *or* offense.

Hope

Each form of despair described by Anti-Climacus is logically convertible to a "not being willing to hope" (eg. *SUD*: 204). Thus "despair over the earthly or over something earthly" is the same thing as not being able to hope for the eternal. "Despair about the eternal" is not being willing to hope for the finite. Defiance— "willing despairingly to be oneself"—is not being willing to hope at all (*SUD*: 201). But that the highest pitch of despair—defiance—is not being able to hope at all indicates that the other forms of despair have some element of hope within them. That those other forms of despair are, despite the presence of hope, nonetheless despair indicates that some ways of hoping are, properly understood—which means understood from the point of view of what Christianity ought to be—illusory. Defiance is, in one sense, closest to the religious because it has no illusory hopes. That is to say, defiance has no hopes that are not grounded in God; the characters suffering from other forms of despair do. But since defiant characters refuse to ground themselves in God they—with the necessity and consistency of syllogism—have no hope at all. Having no hope at all is exactly how things do stand for the natural man—at least that is how Christianity understands the matter. That few human beings understand things that way is an indication of how confused (subject to sin? ... pagan?) most of our thinking about ourselves (our subjective thinking) is.

i) Unconsciousness of despair/Thoughtless hope:
Mr. & Mrs. Lemming

Most people are unaware that they are in despair. That is, most people do not know that their hope is a form of hopelessness. Both Kant and Kierkegaard would agree that a person who hopes only for the finite: "give me a house, a good stereo, two cars and a good looking mate" is bound to failure. Not because finite things are things one can always want more of after getting a taste of them, but because part of the character of a human being is in itself infinitely demanding. That demand such a person is unaware of or has not thought of. Even if this person did win the whole world so that there was no thing left to desire, there would still be the infinite demand.

A person could go through life this way, bound to finite hopes. He might seem happy. He might consider himself so. He would be wrong.[17] Such a character is in despair because what he hopes for cannot possibly be the fulfillment of the self which hopes for it. These characters are the background against which the characters within Kierkegaard's drama play and from which his authorship draws its reader.

There are many ways in which a character may help himself away from the realization that there is after all something infinite or eternal about himself, i.e. that the difficulty of hope is rooted precisely and essentially in himself. But however he manages his despair this particular kind of character is unaware of the fact that all his hopes are vain. All of the other forms of despair share something of this unawareness, but in the other forms some kinds of hopes *are* recognized as vain. In paganism and in the young girl Cordelia Wahl there is only one kind of hope: hope for the finite. This hope is unaware that it is possible to hope for anything else.

ii) Conscious despair over the earthly/
Inability to hope for the infinite:
the poet, Cordelia Wahl

Anti-Climacus diagnoses several types of conscious despair. Among these "A" both illustrates and describes several ways of despairing over the earthly. But the best character to examine here is Cordelia Wahl since she moves via her seduction from unconsciousness of despair to the highest conscious form of despair about the finite. She moves from the background of the drama to the foreground in the play within the play known as "The Diary of the

Seducer" and represents, in a fairly straightforward fashion the
kind of despair that "A" and Johannes, her seducer, attempt to work
around. This first form of conscious despair, a type of "the despair
of weakness," is the kind of despair that all of the "aesthetic"
characters suffer from. It "terminates preferably in the romantic"
(*SUD*: 186). Cordelia prefers to terminate there. Johannes abandons her. Had she a gift for words her last letter to her seducer
might have been immortal:

> When in disgrace with fortune and men's eyes,
> I all alone beweep my outcast state,
> And trouble deaf heaven with my bootless cries,
> And look upon myself and curse my fate,
> Wishing me like to one more rich in hope,
> Featured like her, like her with friends possessed,
> Desiring this man's art and that man's scope,
> With what I most enjoy contented least;
> Yet in these thoughts almost myself despising,
> Haply I think on thee, and then my state,
> Like to the lark at break of day arising
> From sullen earth, sings hymns at heaven's gate;
> For thy sweet love rememb'red such wealth brings
> That then I scorn to change my state with kings
> (Sonnet 29).

As it is, she is not without modulation, though she comes directly
to the point: "Johannes! Is there then no hope at all?" (*E/Or*, I: 309).
The romantic, such as Cordelia, is the clearest characterization of
this "feminine" despair since she puts all of her hope in one person.
Losing this she is not willing to look for anything else, is not able to

hope for the eternal, which hope roots an ethical existence. Cordelia's letter indicates that she has not (as Shakespeare had not) reached the point of defiance—she asks a question about hope, she does not declare that she will not hope for anything. Unlike the poet she is still oriented toward the future; the speaker of Shakespeare's poem takes the back way out of his qualitatively similar despair: memory. Very few people have the spirit to place all of their hopes in one person. It is, of course, shrewd investment policy not to do so. In this way when one hope crashes another finite hope is held on to and so the majority of people unconsciously rotate their hopes within the sphere of the finite.

Having all three of these possibilities—Shakespeare's, Cordelia's, the general run of mankind's—at his fingers' ends so to speak, "A's" first rule, the *sine qua non* for living artistically, is "to abandon hope" (*E/Or*, I: 288). His understanding of what hopes one abandons however is that one abandons all hopes in the finite. This frees the aesthete from bondage to the future. He would see such bondage as the cause of Cordelia's distress—in her last letter she swears she will wait for Johannes. Abandoning hope also frees him from bondage to the past, since there is no special tie to any previous experience—or woman. Such a tie is the source of the torment which underlies Shakespeare's music. If one had hoped for something, then whether it was fulfilled or not it would provide impetus for remembering. Both remembrance and hope distend the present moment and do not allow it its full aesthetic possibilities; both are therefore to be avoided. How "A" got to the point of having this knowledge we don't know. Perhaps it is an innate idea. Cordelia Wahl is brought to this point by her seducer. "A" sees this and becomes uncomfortable. Perhaps it is not an innate idea. Johannes sends back her letters without reading them. How is it that he knows that he does not want to know?

"A's" abandonment of hope allows every experience to be more than one could have hoped for, which is, of course, more than one could hope for from experience. It would, however, be very dangerous for such a one to be asked either where did this wisdom come from? or why not hope in the finite? To the latter "A" might reply, "because you would regret it." But then, why would one regret it? Is that regret necessary? "A" could, I suppose, oil his way around these questions also. But if they were asked by an earnest youth, not Judge William (who cannot be quite so earnest, since he himself has some things he would rather not be asked, and so, expecting politeness, he, out of politeness...), such questions might drive an aesthete, if not to faith, at least into open and admitted defiance. As it is, he dissembles.

A man devoid of hope and conscious of being so, as "A", has ceased to belong to the future. But for "A" this is a pretense. He comes near to voicing the realization that it is a pretense and revealing his true position by revealing what tempts him. What tempts him is the seducer's diary—specifically its title: "*Commentarius perpetuus*." If it had had a more scatological title, say "Cordelia's Seduction," he would no doubt have let it alone.[18] What could have tempted him here in this "running commentary" is the pretense of writing as the events occurred ("described with the dramatic vividness of an action taking place before one's very eyes" (300)). Perhaps even writing them into occurrence. ("His life had been an attempt to realize the task of living poetically; ... he constantly reproduced the experience more or less poetically. His

Diary is therefore neither historically exact nor simply fiction, not indicative but subjunctive" (300).) Subjunctive ... "let there be," and so there is. Writing reality. No supplement, no difference; writing/reality without interruption. *Perpetuus* not *interruptus*. The (wet) dream of signification.

"A" recognizes that Johannes—if the *commentarius perpetuus* is what it proclaims itself to be—has escaped the past and future and so has escaped hope. Its strange title tempts him because if it is true then his friend Johannes has succeeded at what he ("A") ... hopes ... to succeed at: living aesthetically—living without hope. Alive in each moment, but not in time. But a man really devoid of hope and conscious of being so would no longer be a reader—as "A" is.[19] Reading follows a thread, or a skein, into the future. It may follow it for any of a number of reasons—entertainment, enlightenment, distraction, edification—but (and here's the rub which discomforts "A" about the diary—certainly he does not feel guilt) ... but reading makes the reader belong to the future and reveals (fear of revelation is why "A" reads hurriedly, breathlessly—as if afraid of something) that he is not completely without hope. "A" does not ever say this. He does not speak from his hiding place where he reads the (secret?), entrancingly titled diary, but he does cough, fidget, perhaps even (who can tell)—blush. He is only pretending to be devoid of hope.

Johannes, in strict accord with the rotation method which "A" suggested, has other lines out even while seducing Cordelia. Less reflective seducers, having less control, or less knowledge of their lack of control, become manic-depressive. Johannes seeks to precipitate just such a state of manic-depression in Cordelia, who gives herself at the height of her last (and so highest) manic phase. This makes Cordelia's subsequent despair capable of empowering the most radical of changes: dedication to the ethical, suicide, misvironic[20] rage. Johannes says he is preparing her for the ethical dedication required in marriage (perhaps by curing her of romantic attachment to the finite). It ain't necessarily so. It does seem, however, that she cannot stay in the state she exhibits in her last letter except by defiant misvironic rage—which isn't quite what she expresses in that letter. So it seems her choices are the ethical (which is to will to hope for the infinite), the defiant (which is not to be willing to hope at all), or suicide (which is inscrutable, but Anti-Climacus thinks it is not a viable cure for what ails her, since spirit is eternal and a self is spirit and Cordelia is a self). In any case, it is clear when Cordelia leaves the stage that she has been in despair, and that her despair was one which hoped only in the finite.

The seduction, though not represented in the book, brings all of these problems of hope and despair to ... climax and leads even Johannes to give himself away as imperfectly keeping his own advice with the remark "Why can such nights not be longer" (*E/Or* I: 439). That is the unfortunate thing—time holds us, we pass away into it, and know it. *Don Giovanni*—the spirit of sensuality—has no time for such ... regrets. But Johannes realizes that he passes into time, not just through it, and so even the woman's complete giving of herself passes through him and away, and she comes back to herself—different, to be sure (for now, among other things, she is conscious of her despair), but back to herself: passing through the seducer and away—*why can such nights not be longer?* Is time a protection from the seducer? A protection, not in the sense of making one unseducable, but a protective measure in that it disallows completeness to him, even though both desire it.

The problematic character in this inset snippet of drama is Johannes, whom many critics (including Victor Eremita) characterize as demonic. We have just seen that he is slightly less than a perfect demon. He may only be "A's" dream. Certainly he could not succeed in living completely in the subjunctive. That is the prerogative of poetry, not poets. Be that as it may, Johannes exhibits in his activity the Christian claim that the devil, despite himself, does the will of God. Here he is seen preparing Cordelia's legs ... for leaping. The seduction moves the larger drama forward by preparing "A", Victor, and the reader for the next stage. That remark is informed by an understanding of the drama of the authorship as a mystery play. From the other point of view, Johannes' seduction of Cordelia makes it possible for one other person (namely her) to see how well the seduction was laid. This little play within the play shows the discriminating reader what Kierkegaard the seducer is after: The acme of seducers would not glory in the praises of a whole theatre of Leporellos, Leporello hasn't got a feeling for the art of it. 'Tis the judgement of the judicious Johannes plays for. And he must be the tutor of her discretion. So too with Kierkegaard. *De te fabula narratur, kære læser.*

iii) Conscious despair about the eternal/
Not willing to hope for the finite:
Johannes de Silentio, Judge William.

The second form of conscious despair—despair about the eternal—is "despair over one's weakness" and it is this type of despair which is the disease Judge William, if not Immanuel Kant, suffers from.

Kant's argument against despair can readily be seen as one which aims at this second form of the despair of weakness. Like the first form, this despair "does not always come about by reason of a blow, by something that happens, but may be occasioned by the mere reflection [with which] the self becomes aware of itself as something essentially different from the environment, from externalities and their effect upon it" (*SUD*: 187f.). Such an awareness is clearly achieved by the man who recognizes the moral law as a command laid upon him by pure reason. But the same person who recognizes the autonomy of his will in the moral law may well note the thousand ills that flesh is heir to, as Kant himself does (*KU*: 452), and despair of achieving the end commanded by the will (the moral good) which is essentially different from that environment (the amoral). Like Anti-Climacus, Kant would call such despair the despair of weakness, but where the first weakness was one of not knowing that there is a "must", this second weakness lies in the fact that the person has "not learned what "must" means, regardless, infinitely regardless of what it may be that comes to pass" (*SUD*: 190). Such a character attempts to avoid being himself, for in Kant's language what a self is is the moral personality, and when made aware of the infinite difference between himself and the surrounding world caused by being a moral personality this self desires to sink back into the immediate, the amoral realm of nature. But Kant is right here: once aware of his moral personality, this escape is not available. The back door through which this character would like to slink is suddenly too small for him. He is, quite literally, a world too wide for it. He must go forward with the demand of morality or "in his own eyes be a worthless creature," for the moral law *is* his own eyes.

Judge William pretends to have recovered immediacy and the finite (thus marriage can have an aesthetic validity). However, at the same time that he resolves to go forward, despair, without opening the back door, reappears at the front. The resolution to go out into the world in order to refashion it in accordance with the categorical imperative is met at the door by despair which whispers to the Judge that he is too weak to fulfill the infinite demand of morality. The Judge dissembles: "I will do what I can." Despair reminds him: "That is not what must means." Honesty requires that one despair over one's weakness. The Judge dissembles: "Things will work out." Completely clear despair would take the form of not willing to hope that the ethical demand can be fulfilled in the finite. The Judge dissembles. He is "half in obscurity about his own condition" (*SUD*: 181).

Johannes de Silentio dissembles less. He makes no pretense of recovering the finite; he resigns it. He does spend an awful lot of time considering Abraham's teleological suspension of the ethical, though. Why does "his mind [revert] to that story, his enthusiasm [become] greater and greater, and he less and less able to understand the story? [Why], at last, in his interest for that, [does he forget] everything else?"(*FT*: 9). I suggest that he is avoiding something, as Judge William is. He is avoiding coming to terms with the fact that if he has really resigned his hopes in immediacy and the finite, then he has *ipso facto* resigned the ethical life which demands to be carried out precisely in the finite. Abraham is so attractive because it seems he could have led an ethical life (which Johannes can understand, if not live), but he forsakes it for the religious, which Johannes cannot even understand. There was Abraham, who could have what Johannes knows and "knows" to be higher than what he can achieve, and Abraham puts it aside for something higher still. And Johannes knows it must be higher still since he knows what the ethical requires and that no ethical man could—so calmly, so untremblingly—put the ethical aside as Abraham most assuredly does. O marvelous fear and trembling! What longing Johannes must have to touch even the hem of Abraham's cloak; to be even at the point of facing the choice Abraham made! But he is resigned. He, like the Judge, does what he can. Johannes' longing illustrates that resignation is at once the highest ethical achievement as well as the deepest ethical despair: An ethical man who realizes his ethical inadequacy, to say nothing of the religious.

To return to philosophy for a moment: Does Kant dissemble? That depends. In the early moral works—*Foundations, Critique of Practical Reason*—he denies that our intentions are fully scrutable. However, it seems that every moral person, though he may not be sure of his moral goodness, is perfectly aware of times when his maxims are not morally legitimate, his intentions dishonorable. And once a man has broken with the moral law—how dare he then hope for the complete good? With his own moral status no longer in question, but himself convicted, how could he face the just connection of happiness with desert that morality demands with hope, not fear? Isn't it impossible? Isn't expectation of evil fear, not hope? Kant does not take this problem up until the *Religion*. In that book he offers the arguments presented in Chapter Two. Those arguments make it clear that the ethical project needs Atonement, besides the earlier requirements of Just Judge and Eternal Life. A doctrine of Atonement brings with it a bevy of philosophical

problems which either indicate a shift from the original ground of
the ethical project or discover that the requisite atonement is
impossible on the original grounds. This last point has already
been made in the "man to man conversation" which brings the
argument of Chapter Two to a close. That discussion is, originally,
one which is more intimate than that of a lover with his beloved for it
has its beginning on one page in Kant's *Religion*. It has its
beginning seemingly in one voice: Not only are both speakers for
the first two interchanges directly out of the same page of that book,
but, in fact they alternate sentences on that page. The voice of the
interlocutor goes underground after that, but I try to make it clear
that Kant is still answering to his own deep-seated questions. In
other words I have read that section of the *Religion* as a telephone
conversation in which we hear (after the first two interchanges)
only one side of the dialogue. The third voice (Kierkegaard's—
from his dissertation) enters the discussion for two purposes. First,
it exhibits which of the Kant-voices is the one Kierkegaard sides
with, *viz.*, the underground interlocutor. Second, Kierkegaard
makes it clear that both voices can no longer coexist under the same
roof. Kant, in order to remain one person, must cast out one of the
speakers. If he goes with the interlocutor, hope is not *innerhalb der
Grenzen der bloßen Vernunft*. If he goes the second way, there is no
hope for the ethical project because, as noted, it needs atonement. As
we saw in that discussion the problem is not made any easier by
suggesting that morality demands a moral disposition rather than a
clean balance sheet. If Kant wants to hold both that the ground has
not changed and that there is hope, then he dissembles.

My own opinion, as enacted in the discussion, is that he sides
with the voice of Kierkegaard and so essentially Kant and

Kierkegaard agree—not only in the point from which they start (that
there is an essential task and to fulfill it is to become a self), but also
in the way they finally answer (that hope lies on the other side of
pure reason). Kant's writing in the rest of the book does not go that
way, but at the point of the man to man conversation he either must
go that way or despair. I do not think he despairs. I hope that by
bringing out the voice of the interlocutor I make it plain that it is that
interlocutor who is the driving force behind the movements of
Kant's argument. Kant wants to bring that interlocutor around to
his point of view. He has tried any number of ways (the major
movements of which were rehearsed earlier in Chapter Two) to hold
on to his own point of view and at the same time get the interlocutor to
come around. He does not ever throw the interlocutor out or pretend
that his questions are bogus, but treats him like the voice of
conscience whose questions he is constrained to answer. If it is the
voice of the interlocutor which is closest to Kierkegaard's, and that
voice is the conscience of Kant's enterprise, then the dissimilarity
between Kant and Kierkegaard consists in an essential similarity.
As things unravel in the scene the voice of conscience remains very
calm, for it knows that only when things are completely unravelled
will the leap (if ever) be made. By contrast, the voice Kant writes in
becomes like that of a little dutch boy without enough fingers to plug
the dikes—until he finally realizes that if he is not going to drown it
will be due to the grace of a power outside of himself. I may be
mistaken; perhaps Kant does despair. Or perhaps he dissembles.
"The dialectical interplay of knowledge and will" makes the
question about Kant undecidable and "in interpreting [such] a man
one may err, either by emphasizing knowledge merely, or merely
the will" (*SUD*: 181). The reader will have to judge the significance

of that little drama herself.

The Judge, at any rate, is suffering from disease. He is vaguely aware of this fact. At least a bit of dis/ease shows up in the rhetoric of his letters. For example, the last letter to his young friend (who may very well be Johannes, the seducer who prepares young girls for the ethical task of marriage, though "A" protests that he is not) ends this way: "so receive my greeting, take with you my friendship;.... Receive also a special greeting from her whom I love, whose thoughts are concealed in my thoughts, receive a greeting which is inseparable from mine, but receive also a special greeting from her..." (*SV* II: 298; my translation). It may be that his beloved wife's thoughts also conceal something from the Judge, something inseparable from the Judge to be sure—since the two have become one flesh—but something ... special. The Judge clearly has some hope that the infinite demand of morality can be met. Though he attempts to salve his own conscience by "doing what he can" he certainly hopes that his beloved wife did better than that. His young friend might very well have something he could whisper in the Judge's ear that would drive him out of his last place of concealment. That is to say, the seducer—if (over his protestation) his young friend is that—might be able to find out the place where the Judge conceals himself from the fact that the high hopes of his ethical existence are not completely under his control. (Perhaps the seducer has already found that fine and private place.) It would, of course, be impolite to whisper such a thing in the man's ear over coffee in his own house.

It is interesting to note that the Judge has placed himself in his relationship to his wife in a situation analogous to that into which

Cordelia placed herself with Johannes. As Johannes says that he is leading Cordelia to a higher level of consciousness, the Judge says that he is "saved" by his wife (since he must be one of the 99 saved by a woman, not directly by the grace of God). What if her "saving" of him—a claim which she never makes for herself—is based on a previous ... seduction?

The Judge is in a very difficult position. The house he lives in he cannot bring to completion. The walls around him have cracks through which...the wind may whisper. He can continue to hide the fact that he is not really able to hope in the finite, i.e., he can continue to dissemble—agreeing with the philosophers that the unexamined life is not worth living, but spending most of his efforts as an examining magistrate over other people's lives, not quite so much on his own. He could, on the other hand, realizing the impossibility of the task of ethics, defiantly decide that since

> his hopes and fears, his loves and his beliefs
>> are but the outcome of
> accidental
>> collocations of atoms; ... that [since] all the
> labours of the ages,
>> all the devotion, all the inspiration, all the
> noonday brightness
>> of human genius are destined to extinction and
> the whole temple of
>> Man's achievement must inevitably be buried
> beneath the debris of
>> a universe in ruins, ... only on the firm
> foundation of unyielding
>> despair can the soul's habitation henceforth be safely
> built.[21]

It would not pay to examine this defiant credo rationally. It is obviously not a rational credo, composed as it is of oxymoron and paradox. Such a man is obviously more of a poet than a logician. It should, however, be pointed out for the sake of completeness that defiance is, as was pointed out at the beginning, the refusal to hope at all. On the third hand, the Judge could find himself on the other side of a leap.

iv) Hoping all things:

the young man.

Anti-Climacus describes a young man who is educated into hope as it ought to be in *Training in Christianity*, III, 4. His education begins with "a necessary deceit" (184). S. Kierkegaard, religious writer and editor, discourses about affliction awakening, then bereaving, and in the end (but also, always) recruiting hope (*XD*: 114-118; cf. *WL*: 236).

Maybe we ought not go forward with this education. After all, the Seducer described his own task in the same way: The only way for Cordelia to become a woman is through his deceit. Christianity has an ethical explanation for the necessity of its deceit too: the learner has chosen to be in error. Like the young Cordelia who is ignorant of what it means to be a woman, the young man is sick, so that what is healthy food would be regurgitated if it were not spiced to disguise its nature. Christianity and the Seducer are both paternalistic, but Christianity's physic has a kind of force that the Seducer's paternalism cannot match, for Christianity claims that if the young man does not eat of what it offers he will surely die. The Seducer can only say that Cordelia should be led by him because if she is not there are some things that she will never know—she will remain in ignorance. There should be a sign over the path the seducer would like to lead the young girl on that is similar to the one which Victor imagines that the Judge might (but neither actually does) put over the seducer's diary:

> "My fair reader, you will perhaps find in this book
> something you ought not know."

The sign over Anti-Climacus' path would read

> "My beloved friend, there is something here more
> frightening than you can imagine and you do not
> want to know it, but it is required that you do know it,
> for you ought to live according to it."

This, at any rate, is the way Anti-Climacus says things are.

The young man in Anti-Climacus' story goes forward. His imagination takes up "the picture of *that* perfected One whose perfection consisted precisely in the fact of having endured, not only frightful sufferings, but also what is most opposed to perfection (ideality), namely, daily indignity and vexation" (*TC*: 185). There are two deceits possible here. The first—which was the beginning of the apostolic education—was that they were not informed that all those evil things would happen to them. The second—with which our contemporary young man begins—is that the imagination represents the struggle of the perfected One as it represents all things: all struggle, all suffering, all responsibility, all reward—as already completed. But struggle, suffering and responsibility do not exist that way. They are all "too long for a play" and cannot be represented adequately on the stage of the imagination.

So the young man, taken by the picture, desires to resemble it. The die is cast. He dedicates himself to carrying it out in actuality. It was precisely at this point that the seducer took Cordelia and then deserted her. As it was for Cordelia, so now the difficulties for the young man begin. He has begun with the hope of winning through to the glorious conclusion in the finite. Things go badly, he expected this, but he hopes "better times may come" (*TC*: 189). He learns that this hope is deceitful, that all he can hope for is to be hated by the powerful, to be associated with the worst class of people, in fact to be an outcast even among them, to be considered a fool not only by the wise, but by every sensible person. He hopes, now, only to hold out: to live up to the ideal and in spite of the suffering to become perfect. New sufferings torment his soul: Is he acting rightly? Is he doing as the ideal commands? He hopes for forgiveness. He is accused of evil; this he expected. He wonders whether this might not be stupid; he puts that thought aside. Suffering, self-doubt, the accusations of others:

> [Enter Fourth Tempter] ...
>
> "Who are you? I expected 3 visitors, not 4."
>
> "I offer what you desire:...
> Seek the way of martyrdom, make yourself the lowest
> On earth, to be high in heaven."[22]

If it is the Tempter who speaks his hope then "man's life is a cheat and a disappointment" (*Eliot*, 194). A cheat if one were to settle for the lower hopes, a disappointment because this highest hope is either a figment of his own imagination, or one planted by an evil genius. The young man cannot exclude the possibility that it is an evil genius, or his own too active imagination, which has led him to such dire straits. The sign on the road that leads to being a Christian should have said

"Abandon all hope, ye who enter here."

It didn't. Even the warning was deceptive. God help us.

"So it is with the true Christian; in his humiliation he is not supported by the recognition of others," (*TC*: 196) nor by recognition of himself as following the pattern, and "at the very last, at the bitterest moment [he is] deserted by the last support ... by God" (*TC*: 193). It seems then that the difference between the Christian youth, the Judge and Cordelia is that the first has no hope whatsoever, the other two have illusory hopes of one type and another. But does the young man have anything Lord Russell does not have? The young man *could* hope in God—even in the moment when he feels forsaken by God in whom he hopes. He could hope in God, that God is good, that God will make good—both on his promise (that his sins are forgiven) and—by making good on that promise—make the young man good; perfect him. This must be what the Christian hopes for. He hopes as well for everything else. S. Kierkegaard leaves us with this edifying thought:

When once affliction has attained what eternity
wants of it [that the young man hope only in God], the
situation adjusts itself properly; for, though the

> pressure [of affliction] remains, it constantly makes
> itself known conversely as hope, converts itself into
> hope" (*XD*: 117).

This is not simply stupid, it is doubly so. First of all it is stupid to say one hopes in the person who has forsaken him. One could only do so by forgetting that he is forsaken. One can hope in the person one feels forsaken by only by feeling not quite completely forsaken. Either the young man is lying about feeling forsaken or he is hoping via delusion. The second stupidity is that the young man, *e concessis*, has faith: i.e., believes God, believes in God, believes that God makes good. Things cannot ever get as bad as Anti-Climacus says. If he has faith, the intensification of the test never reaches the point where the young man can cry out "My God, my God, why have you forsaken me?" Those straits can only be reached in poetic fictions. If a man does reach those straits in actuality he has not got faith. Both things are not possible at the same time in the same person.

It might be thought that since Anti-Climacus is presenting the ideal, not the actual character of Christianity, we can overlook these discomfiting details, since they are not actual problems of actual Christians. Unfortunately, S. Kierkegaard's "Edifying Discourse," which is by and for actual Christians, bodes no better. Moreover, only a fool would make such a defense. What the ideal case illustrates is that there is no thinkable way to be an actual Christian, and as Aristotle and the Greeks said, what cannot be thought cannot be. Whether or not the Greeks are right is a question I do not presume to decide, I am only following the indications of thought.

Love

1. Were it not for God, the command to love could not be known.

2. Were it not for the command of God, all we could love would be ourselves.

3. Were it not for our neighbor, all we could love of God would be idol.

That is not much capital, but it is enough to fund a short boat ride.

III: THE UNITY OF THE THEOLOGICAL VIRTUES
IN THE CHRISTIAN LIFE

Hope had grown grey hairs,
Hope had mourning on,
Trenched with tears, carved with cares,
Hope was twelve hours gone;
And frightful a nightfall folded rueful a day
Nor rescue, only rocket and lightship shone,
And lives at last were washing away.

———*The Wreck of the* Deutschland, Hopkins

It does not look like this ship is going to float either. Maybe what has gone on so far—Kant's deferral of grounds for hope into impossibility, the breakdown of the hopes of every character in Kierkegaard's drama—maybe all that exhibits the utter recalcitrance of hope to be analyzed, explicated or adequately

represented in language. Perhaps also, then, hope is utterly unjusti-
fiable. One thing seems sure: neither the philosopher nor the poet
can get it right.

But there is one positive thing that S. Kierkegaard and the other
religious writers want to point out about the virtues of the religious
character. That positive thought is that there is a unity of the
theological virtues in the Christian's life. Besides the contradictions and stupidities we have so far, or rather, over all these, put
on love.

We might already be tempted to say of the young man who was
seduced into the attempt to become a Christian, "Look, here is a youth
who has allowed himself to be enticed by his imagination to go too
far out, so that he has become eccentric and ridiculous and does not
fit into reality" (*TC*: 188). "But," Anti-Climacus the idealizing
Christian says, "the power which directs man's life is love," though
"only he who loves Him understands" (178). If such a one can love
God—who has led him to that point—I suppose he could love anyone.
This is, in fact, exactly what Christianity commands: that you love
everyone. *Works of Love* is a discourse that founds itself on just
that command.

Major texts of Kierkegaard's authorship are quite explicitly
structured, as selves are, in two parts sundered by a breach. One
could say that such texts are subsistent either/ors. Such a synthesis,
so regarded, is not yet a self. But regarding the texts in this fashion
allows us to mention some differences in the two weights which are
the parts of those major texts. In *Either/Or, Philosophical
Fragments—Concluding Unscientific Postscript, Sickness Unto*

Death, Repetition, the second part reveals the condition for the possibility of having written, read, understood, the first. This may even be true of SÅK's dissertation. Kierkegaard might well have in mind as his model the Bible, in which, for a believing Christian, the New Testament provides the condition for properly understanding the Old. The implied or actual authors of each of these books—Victor Eremita, Johannes Climacus, Anti-Climacus, Constantine Constantius, SÅK, and God—must already be at the point of view of the second part in order for the first part to be written, since that second part is the *sine qua non* of the first. So these works are all backward in the sense that an actual fragment of life, philosophy, psychological investigation, conceptual or sacred history, is presented before what makes each of them possible is elucidated.

Works of Love, on the contrary, is straightforward. It begins with the command of God. According to S. Kierkegaard's understanding this command is the condition for the possibility of love. Part I lays out the command. Part II explicates what love actually does when it holds fast to the command and does not go off on its own, at which moment it immediately and *ipso facto* ceases to be love. If the first works are to wound from behind by presenting a brilliant aesthetic, philosophical, or psychological fragment and then pointing out the offensive fact that it is not human wisdom but Christian revelation which makes such brilliance possible, this latter work straightforwardly lays down the rigors of the New Law—the offensive law which is so offensive and so without understanding as to command love—but then follows with the romantic lunacy (beloved by all) that love conquers all.

But the first part is first.

The religious writer S. Kierkegaard here presents Christianity as it actually is: all the popular talk about what *caritas* is (what Christianity is thought to be) is true—when it is rooted in the command. Whenever both are not present, neither is true. Both S. Kierkegaard and Anti-Climacus consistently oppose love to self-love. Neither author takes any effort to set up or expatiate upon any other distinction. Love is commanded. Self-love is not. Christianity agrees with natural philosophy that it would be stupid to command self-love since it is natural. It agrees with classical philosophy that friendship is love of a second self, with Aristophanes in *Symposium* that *eros* is a form of self-love, and, in general, with anyone else who will say that all such things that are natural to man are self-love. Anti-Climacus claims that this distinction (love/self-love), like those of faith/despair and hope/despair were not able to be made properly in paganism (*SUD*: 178). The most intelligent pagans agreed: they did not make the distinction—there was only true self-love and false self-love. Nothing else was possible.

S. Kierkegaard picks up this idea and links it to the theme Anti-Climacus sounded as the rebuttal to the charge that the young man is eccentric, ridiculous and unfit for reality:

> No one can hope unless he also loves; he cannot hope for himself without loving, for they are eternally inseparable; but if he loves he also hopes for others. In the same degree to which he hopes for himself, precisely in the same degree he hopes for others, because precisely in the same degree in which he hopes for himself, in precisely the same degree he is a lover (*WL*: 239).

A critic whose name I can no longer remember said of *Works of Love* that it is "highly expressionistic." That may be so. Such things are dangerous in a philosophical text, so in order to protect myself against such poetic license, I will approach the claims which S. Kierkegaard makes in that book with an eye to their logic. The book begins—after a foreword, a prayer and a short expressionistic discourse on the essential hiddenness of love—in the imperative mood: You *shall* love. The entire first part remains in that mood. Let us brush through these leaves, since they hide no fruit and pretend we are obeying the command. Under these pretenses let us follow out *in mente* how things are in that possible world where this command—said to be the will of God—is followed.

As always in logic, we begin with definitions: God = that all things are possible; the completely other; love; the eternal. That the eternal and completely other has revealed himself in time through the completely immanent (as is indicated by the existence of the command in ordinary language) is the paradox. That the paradox is true is assumed at the beginning of this thought experiment.[23] In *Works of Love* Kierkegaard is clearly choosing the affirmative answer to our opening question: whether or not besides philosophy anything else is necessary. Some further definitions which are operative throughout this particular text: God-relationship = an inscrutable relation between the absolutely other and an existing individual. In this relationship the individual attempts to understand himself in and to live in obedience to the will of God. Love = to bring an individual closer to God. *Ergo—*

Love --> Hope for others

First we should take up the command, but here we must note that all
that follows is, in the life of an actual person, temporally preceded by
faith, for without faith one does not acknowledge the demand as
commanded by God.   The command to love one's neighbor commands us to bring her closer to God, but since a God-relationship is
an inscrutably subjective one this seems impossible.   On the
contrary, the command requires two things: 1) To believe that your
neighbor has a God-relationship and is acting in accord with it. 2)
To hope that your neighbor will return to fulfilling (if she is not—
which is inscrutable) or will continue to fulfill God's will for her.
Since a God-relationship is inscrutable and since God is that
everything is possible, knowledge of your neighbor's activities is
completely indecisive.   It is also, in one way, a temptation, for the
command is to love, which implies 1 and 2; it is not to investigate,
which at least means holding 1 in abeyance until the investigation
reaches the point at which 1 becomes, if not certain, at least a fair bet.
So love implies hoping for others; it implies faith in others, i.e., that
they are living in accord with God's will, also.   Faith in others
comes about in an indirect fashion, but means exactly what was
indicated above: When one obeys the command he believes God,
believes in God and believes that God loves each individual, thus
one believes that each individual is in relation to God.

Hope for oneself = Hope for others

One's hope for others takes the same kind of indirect path that one's
faith in others takes.   One is able to hope because God is that all
things are possible. Because of this one hopes for one's neighbor and

if at some time worldly shrewdness tempts you to cease to hope for your neighbor, *ipso facto* you have given up your hope in God, your faith that God is that all things are possible, as well as your love for your neighbor. At first glance this might seem to make faith and hope—if not all three theological virtues—into the same thing. There is a unity of the theological virtues, but they are not the same thing. Insofar as faith believes God, believes in God, and believes that God makes good, it is distinct from hope which is an expectation of the good for both oneself and one's neighbor. But insofar as faith believes that God makes good it is inseparable from the hope which expects the good for both oneself and one's neighbor. If the first (faith) is given up, then the second (hope for both oneself and others) is *ipso facto* given up. If, on the other hand, one does not expect the good for both oneself and one's neighbor, then one lies if he says he has faith. *If I had had more faith...*

By giving up on one's neighbor one has limited what it is possible for God to do, but this subtracts just as much possibility from oneself as from the neighbor, for God after all remains the same. Hope for oneself thus varies directly with hope for one's neighbor. The converse is also a directly varying relation. If one loses either hope for oneself or hope for one's neighbor, then one has ceased to believe in God and that God makes good and so he must immediately resign the hope he wishes to hang on to. Either hope or despair[24] and hope is for both oneself and one's neighbor. Take, for example, Russell's expression of defiant despair. Is it possible for Russell to hope for anything for anyone else? No. He would have to call any such other hopes unwarranted—not real hopes, but illusions. He would see his task as educating people away from hope. Russell is, here, completely consistent for his book attempts to do precisely that. This *educere* Christianity labels *seducere*. Perhaps it is mere accident that his essay begins with a scene from *Faust*. Perhaps it is a warning. For Russell too, one's hope for oneself is exactly equal to one's hope for others.

Hope for oneself = Being a lover

We could utilize the conclusions of the two previous paragraphs to justify our next conclusion, but such use of logic would cheat us of understanding what is going on here. To hope for oneself is to expect the good for oneself. Except for the person who was defiant— expected nothing good, and had no hope at all—all of the characters mentioned earlier expected some good for themselves. Not only did they not and, in the case of the ethical characters, could they not achieve that good on their own power, but the good they hoped for was small in comparison with the eternal. Insofar as the good they hoped for was less than God they did not love themselves. Similarly, insofar as they themselves did not hope in God but in various other things, there were limits to their love for others. I mentioned in passing what one of the Judge's limits in loving his wife might be. Insofar as the one who obeys the command hopes in God and for God, he loves himself, for he hopes for the best for himself and with the best "reason:" God is that all things are possible. Two paragraphs above we noted that the same kind of like for like holds with regard to loving the neighbor: To hope for less than God for the neighbor is not to love her. These arguments should make it clear how Kierkegaard thinks hoping for oneself and being a lover are the same thing.

To return to the start of this piece of explication: the command to love. It seems that since hope and this commanded love mutually imply one another and that since despair and hope contradict one another, the exit from despair must be through obedience to the command. One might be tempted to think that there is an original and correlative disobedience at the entrance to despair.

Faith <=> Love

Faith—believing God, in God, that God makes good—implies love in two ways. First, it requires it: love is commanded by God. Second, it implies it in that if one believes that God makes good, one believes it of the neighbor and that is just what loving the neighbor is. God's making good both allows and commands that one believe the neighbor to be in correct relation to God and hope that she continue to be so. This commanded love is essentially equalizing, the only essentially democratic power on earth. In *Symposium* love is what led a man to love a body, bodies, a soul, souls, and so on, finally to loving beauty itself. *Eros* loves what one can see— actually or in the metaphoric sense of *nous*—until the highest. Then it loves what no man has ever seen, what if he would see, would change him essentially, for then, if ever, it would be given to him to become immortal (212a). In his *Confessions* Augustine said (as any good Platonist would) that the Unseen Beauty led him through the world, himself not really knowing what he searched for. It is only because of faith that he can say that it is God who has led him by his desires through the world. Faith grants the condition for his confession. In *Works of Love* Kierkegaard deconstructs this founding metaphor, these founding texts, of philosophy and theology. If, like the young man, one has faith in God, then one loves God, and then immediately and on the basis of this Unseen

One, he loves every individual. One does not find a beautiful body, then discover that there are many such, or find a beautiful soul, then desire to help make many so. No; immediately every single individual is to be loved. It is not the case that the Beauty that one loves and seeks is not (really) to be found in this world. Love commands that you do find it in this world—in the person next to you. There is nothing left to learn, no new insight waiting higher up. There is no ladder. *Either* life is an act of love *or* it is not an act of faith. S. Kierkegaard says that the pseudonyms chose their own names. It was not accidental that the idealizing Christian writer chose the name "Anti-Climacus:" there is no ladder.

Love implies faith because it is only the commanded love which has the power we have been investigating in this thought experiment. Poets may sing of human love conquering all, but everyone knows they lie and the people who don't know this, or pretend not to know it, are merely giddy. Love requires that you "believe all things;" it requires that you believe in God's saving relation to the neighbor and that every interaction with her be based upon that faith. That love implies faith makes love edifying: love builds up the neighbor by *"presuppos[ing] that love is in the other person's heart, and by this very presupposition he builds up love in [her]"* (WL: 206). This final implication exhibits *Works of Love* as Kierkegaard's most Catholic—in the parochial sense—work. It is clear from this analysis that though faith (temporally) takes precedence—only it allows one to hear the command of love as God's command—one who thinks he has faith without love is lying. And love, as is clear from the title, is *gjerninger*.[24] In fact, it is never ceasing works. There is no such thing as faith alone.

IV: For What May I Hope?

My Love is of a birth as rare
As it is for object strange and high;
It was begotten by Despair,
Upon Impossibility.

——*The Definition of Love*, Marvell

Kierkegaard's name is often linked with Tertullian's and then
both are tossed together on the trash heap of Irrationalism. Of
Tertullian I know little, but of Kierkegaard this is an unphilosophical condemnation. Kierkegaard agrees with Kant that we are
rational creatures; his romanticism, like Kant's, does not extend to
Sturm und Drang depths, and on the other side his passion for
distinctions runs as deep as Kant's, or Socrates'. Socrates too would
admit to being a rational creature, though he would continue to ask
whether he was a being more puffed up with pride than Typhon, or a
simpler, gentler creature whom the gods had blest. Kant attempts to
persuade us to hope that Reason's interests are not illusory, but why
should we believe this creature, which we, in part, are? Isn't it the
most unphilosophical, unsocratic blindness to believe this creature
simply? Especially if we consider that it is divided against itself
and prone to illusions of its own self-divisiveness? Why then *do* we
believe it? Or, since we are no longer of Kant's faith, why do we *not*
believe in its hopes? Does this *credo* or *non credo* have a *quia*? Since
it is a *credo* or *non credo* about Reason's status itself, does it make
sense to ask for a *quia*? To demand one? Or does this question, this
looking for a reason, beg the very question at issue?

Further, what does a philosopher want to point out by making the claim *"absurdum est"*? What motivates such a claim, what passion underlies it? What ... faith? Abraham, by believing the absurd, stood alone—apart from his wife of 50 years, apart from his son Isaac—incommunicado. Believing absurdity makes one an idiot (in the Greek sense: without language). Being made an idiot is a great fear of philosophers. That fear is based on a more general fear latent in every one: the fear of being alone. The passion for community underlies the philosophical cry against *credo absurdum*. Kant makes this point clear by his posing of the epistemological question in terms of communicability. Kant's faith is that there can *only* be a community of *rational* beings; that community can be defined by the phrase "insofar as rational, just so far communal." What is Reason's can belong to all equally, to none as a private possession. Truth, obviously, is this way. The Good too, on Kant's view, might well be this way, for at least what we can know of it—the moral law, pure reason's practical law—is one we all share, and makes us all legislative members of the same kingdom of ends. After Kant, this belief in the community which only exists insofar as it is rational is taken up by Hegel, *blandt andet*, by Hegelians of the right and the left: The rational community splits.

But is it not sometimes the case that human fears are groundless? Or if not groundless, mistaken? How does one discover that a fear is groundless or mistaken? How does one gain a virtue? Say courage, for example? Without a reasoned *quia* ... how does one begin?

By a decision, a choice, and this first choice cannot be made for reasons; to make this first choice for reasons is already to have decided that Reason as it is found in oneself is good enough, its papers valid. But perhaps there is sin, perhaps there is a fault, or a seduction, an original and ineradicable propensity. If there is, then the creature who is unphilosophically reasonable is more puffed up with pride than Typhon, and as doomed and blind about where he comes from as Oedipus. So blind that by refusing to ask the Socratic question about himself as a reasoning being he is turned away from every possibility of learning the truth about that reasoning being which he is. To see such a creature even in imagination evokes terror and pity, that one might be so oneself—

What is most to be feared then: to be an idiot, or to be Typhon and Oedipus together? Perhaps the choice is not quite so stark. When SÅK writes in his diary "I know what they will say—that I know nothing about sociality" (Cf. *WL*: 18) and decides to write *Works of Love* he is presenting to a non-Christian world the possibility of a community not open to a being because of the fact that it exists as a rational creature, *sub specie aeternitatis*, but open to each in her particularity as a self of her own necessities and this possibility: relationship to God as this one. To Reason such a possibility does not exist, because *this one* is incomprehensible as this one—except, perhaps, for Scotists. (And they haven't much to say abut it.)

When S. Kierkegaard is deciding to present *Works of Love*, he does so because he is aware of how his preceding strategy of wounding from behind is likely to work. He knows the human fear of being alone, and so he knows that the response to his wound will be not to turn toward Christianity, but to turn in another way away from it—and with a very good reason ... or is it a rationalization? When someone wounds us with the truth, how many of us are able to turn and embrace it? Of course, then again, this all may be a lie and a seduction.

If Kierkegaard's drama was a mystery play then Søren Å. Kierkegaard himself was engaged in an experiment with Christianity. The experiment did not put a doctrine or a dogma, still less God, to the test. SÅK himself was the subject of the experiment. His own life was the test. It is possible that Christianity is true; it is only possible for you to find out whether or not it is true in one way—by your life. It is possible to lose your life utterly. They say it is also possible to gain your eternal happiness. You are at the parting of the ways; we are where we began:

> Wer hat uns also umgedreht, daß wir
> was wir auch tun, in jener Haltung sind
> von einem, welcher fortgeht? Wie er auf
> dem letzten Hügel, der ihm ganz sein Tal
> noch einmal zeigt, sich vendet, anhält, weilt—,

Or, on the other hand, Kierkegaard could be the *ne plus ultra* seducer.

According to an old tale hope was the one thing that didn't escape from Pandora's box of evils. The happy creator of this story leaves it an open question as to whether Pandora shuts up the one good thing contained in her box or whether she locks in the worst of all evils. Perhaps the writer of the story leaves things that way in order to make the reader decide what she thinks hope is. That would be clever, but in this case it would fail, for about this story I have nothing to say. A feminine reader may want to take another look inside this box to figure out what kind of thing is left inside it.

If hope is the most monstrous of all misshapen things let loose upon the earth, then it would be best to lock that top down, throw away the key. Unfortunately, it is too late; rumour and the latest redaction of Pandora's tale indicate that someone has opened the box again. It is empty. Hope didn't get much description in Pandora's story. The "X" which may limit philosophy hasn't had much analysis in this one. Those two facts are not accidental. After all the imaginable evils had been let loose, one—unimaginable— remained locked in ... for a while. Johannes Climacus suggests that besides everything analyzable and synthesizeable in the phi- losopher's kitchen there might be one thing—the Paradox—locked out. He calls that Paradox the God-Man. Could such a thing be an object for Reason? For imagination? No. It cannot be seen, heard, touched, tasted, smelt. Nor can the heart of man imagine it. Philosophy calls such language empty. There is less referred to by the symbol God-Man than by this one: {}. And look how much follows. If "there was" "such a thing," "it" would "be" utterly uninterpretable. To man, the language using animal, "God" is the "being" who puts all of our words "in suspension." For all x, such that x is a symbol, God implies that x = "x".

The Paradoxical and the monstrous: what reason cannot know nor ghost guess—what philosophy and poetry both keep locked away—that, I suppose, is what hope is. That is what Kierkegaard says the God-Man is. Suppose (to double the stupidity) that the God- Man speaks. Where did these words come from? The 1800 years of scholarship at Kierkegaard's time had not grasped the source. 200

more years have come no closer. An infinitely dedicated scholar in infinite time could not get to the point of grasping even the conditions for the possibility of such a word, much less grasp its actuality. Hermeneutics goes to work on the perfectly ordinary words supposedly uttered by the unbelievable. But everything is different now. There is a shadow of earnestness: if it was—*per impossible*—the God-Man who spoke, and if he spoke (ignoring our natural bent) demanding belief—not commentary, learned *sic et non*, distinctions that could be made—then there is an "authorized version" and to be mistaken about one's interpretation is not only possible (for here authorial intent would not be a fallacy), but also morally damning, for what was demanded was belief—not commentary, learned *sic et non*, theses that could be made. "God amend us, God amend! we are much out o' th' way" (*LLL* IV,iii).

But not to worry. This is all impossible. It might be possible that there is a God, but it is impossible that such a being could really become man. It is just as impossible that God, the absolutely different, could ever speak to human beings. Both are impossible for the same reason: both require that the eternal enter time, the one in word, the other in deed. I don't even know what could have suggested this idea to me. It must have been a dream: man is but an ass, if he go about to expound this dream. Aristotle's silent, unmoved and unmoving mover is the only reasonable way for the eternal to be. And there we cannot hope to enter. Το γαρ αυτο νοειν εστιν τε και ειναι. Then this chapter is full of sound and fury, signifying nothing.

CONCLUSION

15 Theses as Food for After-Thought

1. The dissimilarity between Kant and Kierkegaard consists in an essential similarity.

2. One thing that is always staked in a philosophical text is what philosophy is.

3. "To hope" and "to read" are "to speak metaphorically" the same thing.

4. One begins to hope only by virtue of despairing; one begins to read only by virtue of not reading.

5. There is always more at stake in a philosophical text than the theses within the philosophical text.

6. Every act of understanding as well as every act of will is essentially an act of hope.

7. Hope could be understood as something which only becomes possible after Original Sin, thus a fault would be a condition for the possibility of hope.

8. In that case, moral theory, as well as moral action, since it arises *secundum quid* will not be able to answer its own questions except by virtue of the pretense that it deals with moral problems *simpliciter*.[1]

9. As philosophy begins in wonder, so also that life which is Christian begins in the consciousness of sin.

10. Where philosophy ends in wonder, that life which is Christian ends in the (impossibly unreasonable) hope of redemption and recreation.

11. *Credo quia absurdum* is a more deeply religious confession than *credo ut intellegam* since beneath it lies a confession not of ignorance, but of incapacity.

12. *Either* hope is both impossibly unreasonable (Kierkegaard) and required (Kant), *or* stop reading.

13. "What the poet produces is a verbal object (*poiema*) in which meanings, released from any personal interest he may vest in them, are neither affirmed nor denied, but simply placed. A poem in this sense does not *mean*—it does not urge the feelings and opinions of the poet on the reader. It *is*—as a thing made it is self-sufficient (*perfectum*) and bears no message not indigenous to its perfection."[2]

14. "The nearer [poetic exuberance] approaches actuality, the more it becomes understandable only through a rupture with actuality; the more polemic it conceals in itself, the more it makes a polemical development a condition for the reader's sympathy, slips out of poetic indifference, loses its innocence and acquires a purpose" (*Irony*: 317).

15. "For the conclusion, the disconnected style of language is appropriate, and will mark the difference between the oration and the peroration: I have done. You have heard. You know. Decide" (*Rhetoric* 1420b).[3]

Appendix A

DRAMATIS PERSONAE OF
"KIERKEGAARD: THE AUTHORSHIP"

Søren Aabye Kierkegaard (SÅK) 1813-1855
a.k.a. Magister Kierkegaard after 1841. Engaged 1840-1841
to Regina Olsen.
Author of:
The Concept of Irony, (1841); 21 volumes of *Journals and Papers*, published posthumously. "Credited with" author ship of 14 volumes of *Collected Works*.

S. Kierkegaard (SK)
"From first to last a religious author."
Author of:
(?)*From the Papers of One Still Living*, 1838.
31 *Edifying Discourses*,1843-1850.
2 Articles in *The Fatherland*, 1842-1843.
Three Discourses on Imagined Occasions, 1845.
A Literary Review, 1846.
Works of Love, 1847.
Christian Discourses, 1848.
Three Godly Discourses, 1849.
5 *Discourses at Communion on Friday*, 1849-1851.
For Self-Examination, 1851.
21 Articles in *The Fatherland*, 1854-1855.
This Must be Said; So Let it Be Said Now, 1855.
10 numbers of *The Instant*, 1855.
"God's Unchangeableness," 1855; preached in 1851.
The Point of View for My Work as an Author, 1848.

Publisher of:
all of the above except *The Point of View for My Work as an Author*.

Editor of:
The Sickness Unto Death, Training in Christianity.

"A"   Author of:
Volume I of *Either/Or*, except "The Diary of the Seducer,"
also "A Passing Comment on a Detail in *Don Juan*," in *The Fatherland* (1845).

Receiver of Judge William's letters. Perhaps also the
"young man" who speaks at the banquet in *Stages on Life's
Way*. Perhaps also "the young man" whose story is told in
Repetition, and author of several letters Constantine
publishes there. May also (or otherwise) be Johannes the
Seducer.

A.F.   Author of "Who is the author of *Either/Or*?" in *The
         Fatherland*, 1843.

William Afham
         Narrator of the banquet in *Stages on Life's Way*.

Anti-Climacus
         Author of *Sickness Unto Death, Training in Christianity*.
         Publisher of a discourse given by Magister Kierkegaard in
         "Part II" of the latter book.

"B"   a.k.a. Judge William, author of Volume II of *Either/Or*,
         except "Ultimatum." Also author of "Various Observations
         about Marriage in Reply to Objections" in *Stages on Life's
         Way*. Friend of "A ".

Hilarius Bookbinder
         Editor of *Stages on Life's Way*, 1845.

Constantine Constantius
         An Experimental Psychologist; friend of the "young man"
         (= "A"?) of *Repetition*; author of *Repetition*, 1843; a speaker
         at the banquet in *Stages on Life's Way*.

Victor Eremita
         Publisher of *Either/Or*; a speaker at the banquet in *Stages*.
         Author of "A Word of thanks to Professor Heiberg," in *The
         Fatherland*, 1843.

H.H.   Author of *Two Minor Ethico-Religious Treatises*, 1849.

Vigilius Haufniensis
         Author of *The Concept of Anxiety*, 1844.

Inter et Inter
>   Author of *The Crisis* and *Crisis in the Life of an Actress*,
>   1848.

Johannes Climacus
>   A young philosophy student, hero of SÅK's unpublished
>   novella (or is it a *roman a clef* for the authorship?) *De
>   Omnibus Dubitandum Est*; also author of *Philosophical
>   Fragments*, (1844), *Concluding Unscientific Postscript*,
>   (1846). Ghost author of *The Point of View*? The "young
>   man" in *Stages*?

Johannes, the Seducer
>   Author of "The Diary of the Seducer;" a speaker at the
>   banquet in *Stages*. Acquianted with Judge William. It is
>   not unreasonable to suspect that he is really "A".

Johannes de Silentio
>   Author of *Fear and Trembling*, 1843.

Nicholas Notabene
>   Author of *Prefaces*, 1844.

Quidam
>   A young man whose diary is the first part of "Guilty/Not
>   Guilty," in *Stages*. Perhaps also the young man who speaks
>   at the banquet.

Frater Taciturnus
>   Author of "Guilty/Not Guilty" in *Stages*, "The Activity of a
>   Traveling Aesthetician and How He Still Happened to Pay
>   for the Dinner" in *The Fatherland*, 1845 and "The
>   Dialectical Result of a Literary Police Action," *Ibid.*, 1846.

A woman's tailor
>   A speaker at the banquet in *Stages*.

A Jutland priest
>   Author of "Ultimatum" in Either/Or; friend of Judge
>   William.

Cordelia Wahl
>   Writer of two letters published in "The Diary of the
>   Seducer;" seduced by Johannes; known (in the biblical
>   sense?) by "A." Her last name is fictitious.

Extra-Dramatic Personnel

Regina Olsen
> Beloved of SÅK; ghost author of *Forlovelsen*; perhaps also S. Kierkegaard's *"kære læser;"* person to whom the authorship is dedicated.

Cordelia Olsen
> Sister of Regina; reported to have said of SÅK "After all I believe he is a good man." The last name is not fictitious.

Michael P. Kierkegaard
> Father of SÅK; person to whom the authorship is dedicated.

Peter Christian Kierkegaard
> Brother of SÅK; publisher of *The Point of View;* a bishop in the Danish State Church.

Raphael Meyer
> Friend of Fru Schlegel (nee Regina Olsen); author and publisher of *Forlovelsen*, 1904.

Assistant Professor
> A class of low-life which is parasitic upon the life-blood of original artists and thinkers; similar to Priest (see below). The writer of this book is one example.

Priest
> A class of low-life which transubstantiates the life-blood of God and his martyrs into a good living.

A typesetter
> One who requested that S. Kierkegaard keep the "Preface" to his first series of *Edifying Discourses*; perhaps also S. Kierkegaard's *kære læser*.

Governance
> Director of the authorship according to S. Kierkegaard.

Mr. X, Esq.
> The real reader of Constantine Constantius' book, *Repetition*, and the one to whom he addresses it in a concluding letter; a fictional character.

Appendix B

WHAT OTHER BEINGS ARE PERSONS?

In "Kantian Knowledge of Other Persons—An Exploration" [*Akten des 4. Internationalen Kant-Kongressus*, Teil II.2 (Berlin: Walter de Gruyter, 1974): 576-781], H. Tristram Engelhardt argues that we can have no experience and therefore no theoretical knowledge of persons as moral agents. "Strictly, the world as presented in objective experience is free of persons" (580). Therefore we can only confer personhood on an object of experience by analogy to ourselves. This argument seems to move Kant's moral philosophy too close to the Cartesian problem of other minds and seems to deny that morality can be for all *rational* beings, since we could only recognize those that are "physically similar to [ourselves], as [having] the sort of body one could expect to be "inhabited" by a mind."

I think that this must be incorrect. In *KU* Kant defines a physical end as one the parts of which both are "only possible by relation to the whole" and "combine of themselves into the unity of the whole by being reciprocally cause and effect of their form" (§ 65). This view of objects is based on analogy to reason's view of moral subjects in a kingdom of ends where the same two factors must be true of everyone in the kingdom. To think ourselves as part of a kingdom of ends is, consequently, only possible by relation to the whole in which we are already members in reciprocal interaction. It is not possible to go so far as to doubt that there are other members, which would be the analogue in Kant's moral philosophy of the Cartesian problem of other minds. It is impossible to have this

problem in any way like the forceful manner in which it appears in
Descartes because Kant has tied all conviction—and here we are
speaking of moral conviction—to communication.   Practical
reason's solution to the problem posed by understanding here could
run like this: Any being which can be treated as a member of the
kingdom of ends ought to be so treated. The only kinds of being that
can be so treated are (a) beings with whom we can possibly
communicate, because the others are not possibly "in relation to the
whole kingdom of ends." And they are not so because it is not
possible that they are in relation to us. Perhaps the reasonable test
for possibility here is that the being in question be an originator, an
inventor, of communication, that is to say, the one who attempts to
bridge the gap. So far as I know none of the great apes have made
any attempt to communicate with us. They have no universities
where they cage sample humans and try to teach them how to say
banana. The second Kantian requirement would be (b) that the
beings in question not be creations of human art, because beings
which are such creations do not "combine of themselves into a unity
of the whole by being themselves reciprocally the cause and effect of
their form." Thus, for two different reasons, the most intelligent
computer is no more a moral agent than a stone. (Which latter are
only moral, though not yet agents, if one finds sermons in stones,
books in the running brooks, and good in everything (*AYL* II,i).

Notes to Proem

[1]I have been aided in my wondering by Sylviane Agacinski's *Aparté: Conceptions and Deaths of Søren Kierkegaard*; see in particular the first section "On a Thesis." See also Jacques Derrida "The time of a thesis: punctuations," *Philosophy in France Today*, edited by Alan Montefiore, Cambridge: University Press (1983), 34-50.

[2]John Caputo, *Radical Hermeneutics*, 73.

[3]Some, of course, continue to be perverse. See, for example, Christopher Norris, *The Deconstructive Turn*, ch. 4 and Louis Mackey, *Points of View: Readings of Kierkegaard*, ch. 7.

[4]See Appendix A: Dramatis Personae of Kierkegaard: The Authorship.

[5]Compare, for example, Johannes Climacus' interpretation of Lessing in *CUPS*. The word "blick" is from R. M. Hare's part of "The University Discussion," (*Readings in the Philosophy of Religion*, edited by Baruch Brody, Englewood Cliffs, New Jersey: Prentice-Hall (1974)), by it he means a fundamental world picture.

[6]That the clearest presentation of this system is given by an imaginary character in the "Appendix" to the *Unscientific Postcript* to *Philosophiske Smuler* ought, at least, to give one pause. That the writer of the essay is himself not a systematic philosopher, but rather a humorist, and in addition, a humorist whose *plaisance* is to make things difficult and whose *plaisanterie* is at the expense of systematicians and philosophers ought to make a systematizing philosopher stand completely still.

[7]This discovery which S. Kierkegaard made—that he was a religious author, indeed, from the very beginning a religious

author—was, of course, made before SÅK died. The confession of this discovery is, however, of questionable origin, for the confession (*The Point of View*) is not published until after SÅK's death. The confession then can certainly not be credited to any living person, except, perhaps, Peter, as Louis Mackey seems to suggest in his latest book (*Points of View*).

One might ask whether that confession can be credited to anyone who ever had been living. Only if SÅK and the S. Kierkegaard who wrote it are the same. Here the law of identity is of no help: we must leap to the conclusion that they are the same ... or that they are different. Even if one has legs for making this small leap there are still two problems about trustworthiness. As Anti-Climacus says "it is true that there is rest in the grave; but to sit beside a grave, or to visit a grave—all that is not to lie in the grave; to scan again and again the production of one's own pen, which one knows by heart, the inscription which one placed there oneself and which the man himself can best understand, telling who lies buried there—that, alas, is not to lie buried there oneself" (*TC*: 17f). Then there is the additional problem raised by the fact that the claim made by S. Kierkegaard (= SÅK ?) is a religious one. For Augustine a confession is a public act of faith. If *The Point of View* is taken as SÅK's act of faith, it is an act from beyond the grave. Such an event may be fraught with religious symbolism, but to the plainer understanding an "act of faith" which takes place after death is not an act at all.

[8]*Folovelsen*, udgivne for Fru Regine Schlegel af Raphael Meyer, Kjobenhavn: Gyldendal (1904): p. iv (my translation).

[9]I have been unable to recover this quotation, and so I wonder whether my poor translating skills in my first visit to Copenhagen

led me to be deceived about what is written. However, this I can find in the diary after the incident mentioned above: "But now the affair is really ended. *And never have I felt so light and happy and free about this matter, so totally myself again, as just now after making this sacrificial step! For now I understand that I have God's consent to let her go and to take care of myself, only fulfilling her last prayer: sometimes to think of her and in this way reserving her to history and eternity* (X-2 A211/#6539, italics in original). This phrasing too, is problematic, for what K. could be sacrificing by writing to Schlegel is mysterious. It is quite clear however that his feeling of release could come about by putting the responsibility for the continuance of the temporal break between himself and Regina on Schlegel: *Det bliver hans Sag* (it is his affair), he had written earlier. This scapegoating of Schlegel effectively makes him into a mere parenthesis in the one, true, eternal love story—Søren and Regina.

[10]It should be noted that part of *Either/Or* has this very title, "First Love." A woman never forgets her promises to her first love.

[11]Cf. the epigram of *FT*: "What Tarquin the Proud said in his garden with the poppies the son understood, but not the messenger."

[12]Roland Barthes, *A Lover's Discourse: Fragments*, trans. by Richard Howard (New York: Hill and Wang, 1978) 192. I might have quoted more of this essay, but it would have started to run into money. Just one more piece:

> [The mythologist's] speech is a metalanguage, it
> "acts" nothing; at most it unveils—or does it? To
> whom? His task always remains ambiguous,
> hampered by its ethical origin. He can live
> revolutionary action only vicariously: hence the

self-conscious character of his function, this
something a little stiff and painstaking, muddled
and excessively simplified, which brands any
intellectual behavior with an openly political
foundation ("uncommitted" types of literature are
infinitely more "elegant"; they are in their place in
metalanguage), 146.

[13]Historical footnote: Regina burned all of her letters to SK
when they were given back to her along with what remained of SK's
estate, which he had bequeathed to her.

[14]According to Walter Lowrie's *Kierkegaard*, New York:
Oxford University Press (1938): 224.

[15]Hegel's adaptation of a poem by Schiller. The closing
lines of both *The Phenomenology of Spirit* and Schiller's poem.

[16]Cf. *CUPS*: Appendix: A Glance at a Contemporary Effort.

[17]Roland Barthes, "Myth Today," in *A Barthes Reader*
(New York: Hill and Wang, 1982) 147.

[18]A fragment of this section was published earlier in the
first chapter of my short book *Works of Love?: Reflections on
Works of Love*, (Potomac, MD: Scripta Humanistica, 1990).

[19]Thomas Aquinas, *Summa Theologica* I-I, q.1, a.1; II-II,
q.2, a.3.

[20]Harry Nielsen, *Where the Passion Is: A Reading of
Kierkegaard's* Philosophical Fragments, Tallahassee: Florida
State University Press (1983).

Climacus calls his setting out of the problem of the
Fragments "algebraic" because he is setting out relations between
points of view without making ontological commitments to either of
them. The central concepts—e.g., "the Truth," "Error"—are
"taken to signify the same thing for all men, but [their] content is
left unspecified" (p. ix). Cf. also Louis Mackey who translates

Climacus' algebraic presentation of the problem into a semiotic presentation in *Points of View*: 107.

Notes to Chapter 1

[1]The remarks which follow should be taken in a completely general, algebraic fashion. They are applicable then to any being for whom a task is seen as essential. So, for example, they would apply to such diverse thinkers as Marx—for whom to embody the freedom of the idea in the material economic world is the essential task—and Nietzsche, who seems to think that human beings have a task essentially—to be a bridge for the overman. The distinctions which follow in this discussion will recur—in translation as it were—in every such philosophy.

[2]Some people read *Hamlet* as such a play: Hamlet is given an impossible, because contradictory, but inescapable, because assigned by a greater power (the ghost of his father), task. The task engenders his leading passion and directs the tragic action. It may be that in the three hours of the play "he travels the whole course of the dead end path that the man in the audience takes a lifetime to cover" (Albert Camus, *The Myth of Sisyphus*: 59). That is not the only interpretation available about what happens in *Hamlet*, or a man's life. It is, however, clear, powerful, cogent, and provokes infinite terror.

[3]I suppose it is possible for a being to have more than one essential task. But the ontological complexity of such a being could be simplified by showing that its singular task as the being it is is the accomplishment of all those sub-tasks at once. Then we return to the top of this paragraph: It is possible that there are impossible

essential tasks, i.e., tasks which are a complex of contradictory subtasks. Hamlet seems to be given such a complex by the ghost: revenge your father's murder, and

> let not the royal bed of Denmark be
> A couch for luxury and damned incest.
> But howsomever thou pursuest this act,
> Taint not thy mind, nor let thy soul contrive
> Against thy mother aught" (I,v: 82-86).

4This is Anti-Climacus' definition for a self (*SUD*: 146). Another relation he examines (besides possibility to necessity) is finitude to infinitude.

5Matthew Arnold, "Dover Beach," ll. 35-38.

6John Caputo, "Telling Left from Right: Hermeneutics, Deconstruction, and the Work of Art," *Journal of Philosophy* 83 (1986): 679.

7Cf. St. Thomas Aquinas, *Summa Theologica* I-II Q.22, a.2; Q.26, a.2.

8There may be some doubt as to whether or not Kant would agree with the definition of passion given and on which Kierkegaard and Thomas seem to agree, for he says in the *Religion* that what is "properly" (85) called a passion is "a stage in the faculty of desire [in] which an inclination excludes mastery over oneself" (24n). However, he is certainly aware of my more general use (as his footnote shows) and it is traditional (which is why he feels the need to clarify his own idea). His definition is interesting since it sets in high relief a point which holds true about passions implicated by an essential task: It would be true that such a passion would exclude mastery over oneself, since the task *is given* and since it is the task which arouses the passional dialectic of hope/despair, it is, in that way, not the self which has mastery, but the task.

[9]Since Kant's notion of Reason is complex I have adopted the following shorthand throughout this text in order to keep some of his distinctions working: (R)eason will be used to refer to the undifferentiated rational faculty. That Reason includes understanding, practical reason and judgement. The other reason—(r)eason—will refer to Reason in its practical use, as distinct from Reason's speculative workings.

[10]So we are left single and celibate, as was Kant himself: philosophy imitates life.

[11]"Art" here is meant in its distinctively modern sense as opposed to the sense it has for the Greeks (*techne*). This sense is, naturally, post-Kantian.

[12]The way Kierkegaard puts the same point is like this:

> Cannot consciousness then remain in immediacy? This is a foolish question, for if it could, no consciousness would exist. If this immediacy be identical with that of an animal, then the problem of consciousness is done away. But what would be the result of this? Man would be an animal, or in other words, he would be *dumb*. That which annuls immediacy is therefore speech. If man could not speak, then he would remain in immediacy. J.C. thought this might be expressed by saying that immediacy is reality and speech is ideality (*DODE*: 148).

[13]Or we could use the term already made available by the history of philosophy after Kant—Absolute Knowing.

[14]This predicament is "a contingent and inexplicable fact" according to Beck (*A Commentary on Kant's* Critique of Practical Reason: 50). Kant has a tendency to want to give the inexplicable a moral explanation as in, e.g., *FMM*: 396, *KU*: 433-436.

[15]The view of Kant outlined thus far and which will present
the moral philosophy as the heart and motive for the critical project
is in substantial agreement with the view presented by Richard
Kroner in *Kant's Weltanschauung*, trans. John E. Smith (Chicago:
University Press, 1956). Allen Wood in *Kant's Moral Religion*,
(Ithaca: Cornell University Press, 1970), and Susan Meld Shell in
The Rights of Reason: A Study of Kant's Philosophy and Politics
(Toronto: University Press, 1980) argue for and from a similar
understanding. So, I think, did Kierkegaard.

Kant himself states it fairly clearly even in his major
theoretical work: "I have therefore found it necessary to deny
knowledge to make room for faith" (B xxx). "It is always only to
pure reason, though only in its practical employment, that we must
finally ascribe the merit of having connected with our highest
interest a knowledge which reason can think only, and cannot
establish, and of having thereby shown it to be, not a demonstrated
dogma, but a postulate which is absolutely necessary in view of what
are reasons own most essential ends" (A 818/B 846).

[16]John V. Smyth, *A Question of Eros: Irony in Sterne,
Kierkegaard, and Barthes* (Tallahassee: Florida State University
Press, 1986), especially the chapter entitled "Erotic Economy".

[17]There is, of course, that famous parody, "Dover Bitch," by
Anthony Hecht—but there again it's still the man, imagining the
man, imagining the woman.

[18]A820/B848-A831/B859: "Canon of Pure Reason," section 3.
The example which follows in my text (2+2=5) is not one which Kant
would have used. He thinks that mathematical truths are one and
all *a priori* synthetic and one can tell by conjunction of Reason and
pure intuition that Big Brother is lying. Many modern thinkers

disagree that mathematics is made of *a priori* synthetic propositions. This means then that the propositions of mathematics must either be analytic—a position which Kant himself argues against (B 14-17)—or that they are of the same sort as this: "Oceania is now at war with Eastasia. Oceania has always been at war with Eastasia." In *1984*, it seems that all truths are considered to be of the same kind, none of them necessary. If it were true that there are no necessary synthetic truths, Winston's case would be entirely possible. As it is, there is something not quite believable about the fiction. Perhaps the failure of *1984* to be completely convincing as a fiction in this regard (where we begin by suspending disbelief) is an indication that there are some synthetic *a priori* (necessary) truths. Then the only perfect and complete form of mind control is death. Many modern politicians have become aware of this.

[19](A820/B848, emphasis mine). The prime example of such a truth would be a truth of logic. This is clearly a classical distinction given a Kantian twist. The distinction is that between rhetoric (or poetry) and dialectic (or philosophy), and Kant is drawing the Platonic line with it. Kant connects rhetoric and persuasion explicitly at the end of *KU* (462), connecting both of them in turn with the "popular expediency" Plato complained of as well. The domain of conviction is "an island, enclosed by nature itself within unalterable limits. It is the land of truth—enchanting name!—surrounded by a wide and stormy ocean, the native home of illusion" (A235/B294), the territory of persuasion. If the distinction between persuasion and conviction cannot be held, then the distinction between poetry and philosophy cannot be held on critical grounds any more than it could be held in Plato's *Republic*.

[20]Henceforth "persuasion" and "conviction" will be used in

Kant's technical sense: Persuasion is a judgement thought valid on a ground peculiar to the subject, which ground is, however, thought to be objective (i.e. universally applicable to all subjects). Conviction is a judgement thought valid on grounds of universal subjectivity (i.e. objective grounds), A820/B848f.

[21]A498/B526, emphasis Kant's. Aristotle's realist epistemology achieves the same effect by holding that what senses is potentially like what is sensed (*De Anima* II, v) and that matter is infinitely divisible, but not infinitely divided (*Physics* VI, i).

[22]Roland Barthes says "what is precisely lacking in science ... could be summed up in one word: irony" (Quoted by Smyth *op. cit.*: 265). This state of affairs, in which science becomes ironic has been imagined by Borges in a short story, "The Immortals." I owe thanks to B. David Smith for a showing me this story.

[23]The Kantian explanation of the world we communicate in *a priori* should be contrasted with Peirce's idea of Secondness and Hegelians generally, who (against Kant's admonitions) subject the practical to theory, and as a result consider the formation of the ethical community along the same lines as that of the scientific community. That is, morality for Hegel *et al.* comes to be out of working in the world,rather than being a "condition for the possibility of" human activity. On Kant's view something of the Good is in us; this something—the moral law—though it appears as a demand and a necessity, is, first of all, *enabling*: because of it morality is possible. There is, then, a sovereignty of the good in Kant, though not in Hegel (or in pragmatism). More on this shortly.

[24]This question is one on which Kant seems to change his opinion, as Silber points out in his introductory essay to *Religion*

(lxxxv). It seems to me that Kant's most sensible position is that it is impossible for a finite rational creature to cease to see the moral law as binding him. That's what the deduction in *KPV* is to prove. We cannot make ourselves completely into beasts, though perhaps insanity is that state. But such insanity is not merely moral turpitude; it would infect the subject's entire world. The only unity of the world is moral.

[25]This seems to imply that we cannot know for sure if there are other such free minds out there, but also that it does not matter, for where it is possible to think oneself as free, the moral law is necessary. Kant himself sometimes speaks of the certainty he has in the moral sphere as a kind of here *I* stand, *I* can do no other kind of certainty (A829f/B857f; *KPV*: 144). This is the rationalist, Cartesian side of Kant. We do commonly have a weak type of Cartesian solipsism here, for in the moral sphere we commonly believe it to be the case that another's conscience can neither guide nor truly judge our own. Moreover, like Descartes' cogito (under one reasonable interpretation of it), there is no deduction of the moral law, rather there is an analytic sifting down to it in the *Foundations*, and, in the second *Critique*, it is called an apodictic *a priori* from which other things may be proven. Descartes had reached the Cogito by a similar sifting, and sometimes called the cogito an innate idea, always apodictically certain and useful as a premise from which other things were to be proven. (See "Appendix B" for a stronger argument about Kant's problems with Cartesian doubts in his moral philosophy.)

[26]As Kant says it: "Philosophy is the science of the relation of all knowledge to the essential ends of human reason.... Essential ends are either the ultimate end or subordinate ends which are

necessarily connected with the former as means. The former is none other than the whole vocation of man and the philosophy which deals with it is entitled moral philosophy" (A840f/B868f).

[27]"The idea of a moral world has therefore objective reality, not as referring to an object of intelligible intuition..., but as referring to the sensible world viewed ... as being an object of pure reason in its practical employment" (A809/B837).

[28]Additional correspondences in argument form, etc. are pointed out by Allan Wood: "The Practical Postulates," Chapter Four in *Kant's Moral Religion*.

[29]This is the "Antinomy of Practical Reason,"*KPV*: 115.

[30]In a similar vein Beck notes "Science is limited in two respects: a boundary is fixed beyond which it cannot aspire, and the possibility is established that natural law is not the only formula of causality" (*A Commentary on Kant's* Critique of Practical Reason p.26), though he must mean that critique fixes the boundary of the *legitimate* aspirations of science, since the fact that theoretical reason does in fact aspire (and illegitimately) beyond its boundary is the source of all the antinomies of Reason.

[31]"A final end is simply a conception of our practical reason and cannot be inferred from any data of experience for the purpose of forming a theoretical estimate of nature, nor can it be applied to the cognition of nature" (*KU*: Section 88, 454).

Notes to Chapter 2

[1]There are three kinds of practical imperative according to Kant (*FMM*: 414f). A hypothetical practical imperative, e.g., "if you want to write on Kant and Kierkegaard you should learn *ein*

Bißchen Deutsch og en lille smule dansk" has an end which is wholly optional; the task may be given up. An assertoric practical imperative holds if there is an end which is granted: "Since you want to be happy, you should bribe some reviewers into giving high praise to this book." A categorical practical imperative is the only properly moral one: "You should tell the truth" (no ifs, sinces, buts, ands).

[2]Here most of the Marxists agree with Kant, the disagreement is about what the *telos* is. But any legitimate argument between Marx and Kant must take place at a level transcending that of mere empirical investigation since that kind of reasoning only works through efficient causal chains, and is incapable even of achieving the idea of an end, much less creating one, or deciding upon one.

[3]Cf. Warner Wick, "Truth's Debt to Freedom," *Mind* 73 (1964): 527-537.

[4]To name the most famous—Schopenhauer, Erich Adickes and T. M. Greene think this way. Allen Wood (*Op. cit.*) mentions several others (p. 38-39).

[5]That is, the critical philosophy must meet the canons of objectivity which "characterizes knowledge and distinguishes it from mere fancy and error, to wit objectivity as universality and necessity, produc[ing] a standard for all knowing minds" (Beck, *A Commentary on Kant's* Critique of Practical Reason: 22).

[6]A. J. Ayer's attempt to relegate metaphysics to the boundless seas of meaninglessness is, by comparison, a very stilted attempt to draw the same Platonic line between rhetoric and dialectic; see *Language, Truth and Logic* (New York: Dover, 1952).

[7]To give a Kantian analogy: The two kinds of practical

necessity talked of here are like duties. Duties are one and all
moral necessities, but there are two levels of necessity—a necessity
due to the fact that a maxim cannot even be thought without
contradiction, and a necessity due to the fact that the maxim would
cause a finite will to contradict itself. The moral end of worthiness
is like the former (perfect) duty. The end of happiness is like the
latter (imperfect) duty (cf. *FMM*: 424).

[8]Cf. Gilles DeLeuze, *Kant's Critical Philosophy* (Minneapolis: University of Minnesota Press, 1984), who describes critique
as an "exorcism" of the effects, but not the cause, of illusion on pages
25 and 38.

[9]There are, of course, (to refer Kant back to more
contemporary literature) anti-hero possibilities latent in such a
flawed self. Such a self could choose what seems to lead to happiness
rather than what duty commands; he could be heteronomously
determined. But the idea of happiness is a spineless notion—it flops
in many contradictory directions, and reason, as Kant says (*KPV*:
37, *TP*: 286), is often more hindrance than help in discovering
happiness' true direction. While the protagonist of such a story may
experience much, the character himself could only be seen as petty
and utilitarian. If the society around him were petty and utilitarian
this fault might not show up so starkly, but nonetheless he would be a
petty and unworthy being, and necessarily merely utilitarian.
This option too, has been actualized in post-Kantian philosophy.

[10]See *KU*: 338, where Kant presents this problem as "The
Antinomy of Taste."

[11]Cf. *Summa Theologica* Q. 76 a.2 obj. 3 (*et passim*)
"whatever is received into anything must be received according to
the condition of the receiver."

[12]Cf.*KU* §56 for Kant's definition of these terms.

[13]"Just as, on the one hand, we limit reason lest in leaving the guiding thread of the empirical conditions it should go straying into the transcendent, adopting grounds of explanation that are incapable of any representation *in concreto*, so, on the other hand, we limit the law of the purely empirical employment of the understanding, lest it should ... declare the intelligible to be *impossible*, merely on the ground that it is not of any use in explaining appearances" (A563/B590).

[14]Northrop Frye, *The Anatomy of Criticism*, (Princeton: University Press, 1957): 139.

[15]As Tarski shows, in "The Semantic Conception of Truth and the Foundations of Semantics," *Journal of Philosophy and Phenomenological Research*, 4 (1944): 341-375, a question about the truth of a formal system is always a question which extends beyond the limits of a formal system and so can only be answered from a system which completely includes the system from within which the question is originally framed. Frye gives an analysis of the kinds of symbolic system possible and their hierarchical organization, and Kant exhibits how the question of truth gets displaced from one kind of system to another. (That, of course, is to arrange yet another kind of hierarchy.)

[16]Cf. above, pp. 56f and 107 and note 18 to Chapter 1. This phrase should be contrasted with "universally subjective validity" credited to the categories in the first *Critique* and to the moral law in the second.

[17]These are the titles of the main sections of *FMM*.

[18]See John R. Silber's analysis in the "Introduction" to Greene and Hudson's translation of the *Religion*, pp cv,f. He

follows Kant's usage in the *Religion, passim*. See also *DV*: 213.

[19]Kant's adjective for it, cf. *Rel*: 21, 23, 38, 40.

[20]Contradiction—the source of the passion of a thinker, as Johannes Climacus will say. Kant's contradiction is here in the moral philosophy, here at the root of his third question—for what may I hope? Hope is the passion driving the critical project.

[21]"What was that footnote to our conversation for?"

[22]Pay no attention to it, it's just the man behind the curtain.

[23]Alan Gewirth makes a similar point the basis of his moral theory in *Reason and Morality*, but he does not give his theory the *absolutely* necessary grounding which Kant's transcendental deductions give his theory. He argues instead, as he absolutely must, both that absolute necessity of the Kantian type is impossible and that there is yet a necessity in the conditions of *human* rational willing.

Notes to Chapter 3

[1]One could write a whole dissertation on this topic, as for example, Harvey Hix, "What part ob yu iz deh poEM? Authorship and Authority in Interpretation," University of Texas, 1987 (soon to be published in a revised version as *Morte D'Author: An Autopsy* by Temple University Press). Or at least several scholarly articles, as Roland Barthes "From Work to Text," in *Textual Strategies: Perspectives in Post-Structural Criticism*, edited by Josue V. Harari, Ithaca: Cornell University Press (1979): 73-81 and "Authors and Writers," in *A Barthes Reader*, edited by Susan Sontag, New York: Hill and Wang (1982): 185-193; Michel Foucault, "What Is an Author?" *Journal of Philosophy* LXXXIII (1986): 141-160; Alexander

Nehemas, "What an Author Is," *Ibid*: 685-691; Hugh J. Silverman, "Authors of Works/Readings of Texts," *Ibid*: 691-693.

    In case Kierkegaard is not just playing hide and go seek in his authorship, it is important to consider the question of authorship with regard to it. But even if Kierkegaard's use of pseudonymity is just a Chinese puzzle game allowing him to speak as Tarquin did to his son—in such a way that the assistant professors and thesis writers understand nothing, but that *his* reader loses not a word— even in that case, the authorship of SK raises the question about what an authorship is. And perhaps it gives an answer: A game of hide and go seek.

    [2]The first problem is invoked by literary critics as the "intentional fallacy," the second problem is raised by post-structuralism.

    [3]To say a 'ship is like a ship is no more helpful than to say it is an x.

    [4]Frye, *Anatomy of Criticism*.

    [5]Kant defines love as "the free integration of the will of another into one's maxims" (End: 338).

    [6]Augustine, *De Doctrina Christiana*: III, 10, 14.

    [7]See "Appendix A" for complete list of *Dramatis Personae*. "Kierkegaard" will continue to be used to refer to the whole drama and, indiscriminately, to points that may be made within the drama by any of the characters, or that may be inferred from interactions between them.

    [8]The *locus classicus* here is the play within the play in *Hamlet*: The inset moves the drama along by catching the conscience of the king. The play also presents, in its stock manner, aspects of Claudius' character (for example, the latter is like the

player king in that he is a cunning murderer—but Claudius is not merely that since he attempts remorse).

[9]A more mundane example of a thing with the same literary function is the footnote. It furthers the argument by clarifying one side of a dialectical point within it. Shakespeare is more artful because he puts both the play and the directions for the players within the drama. A footnote, on the other hand, separates the inset from the text. If a writer would write an essay about reading his work within the text of the work it would be considerably more artful than putting it apart from the work in a footnote or in an *ex post facto* explanation, or, for that matter, in a preface.

[10]"The requirement for being a Christian is strained by the pseudonym to the highest pitch of ideality;" hence the pseudonym presents Christianity as it *ought* to be. "Yet the requirement ought to be uttered, plainly set forth and heard. There must be no abatement of the requirement" implies that Christianity as it is *thought* to be silences, dissembles, abates the requirement, "not to speak of the suppression of it." Finally by "making admission and acknowledgement on [my] own behalf ... that I might learn not only to take refuge in "grace," but to take refuge in such a way as to make use of 'grace,'" S. Kierkegaard confesses how Christianity *actually* exists in him (*TC*: 7).

[11]S. Kierkegaard discloses, in his "Preface" to the *Edifying Discourses* that the difference between "edifying" discourses and addresses "for edification" is that someone who gives a sermon for edification has both the authority to build up and a doctrine or *telos* to which he is building. Johannes Climacus concurs (*CUPS*: 229f, 240-44), holding that while everything edifying produces a kind of fear (which stirs the reader/hearer), what is "for edification" stirs by

commanding a certain movement. When on one occasion S. Kierkegaard does publish addresses (*Foredrag*) for edification, he wonders whether there is any audience before whom he pulls it (*XD*: 231f). What kind of address addresses and commands no actual person? No actual address at all. So, are these truly "Addresses—for edification"?

[12]For instance, what other philosophy student has been dialectical enough to make fun of his major professor throughout his dissertation and not only pass his defense, but do so in that same professor's conspicuous absence?

[13]Lowrie remarks in the "Introduction" to his translation of *Attack upon Christendom* that S. Kierkegaard's last publications are "vigorously one sided" and that SK himself was "no longer dialectical." Yet it seems to me that their name and almost savage tone clearly indicate his thoroughly dialectical purpose in publishing them. Further, his style—biting satire at the last—does not evaporate the infinitely dialectical content of his thought, but makes his distinctions stand out more sharply: the lush vegetative "digressions" of *Either/Or* and other earlier—mostly misunderstood, he says—works are cut away. Even if Lowrie is right, he is only right about S. Kierkegaard, who is just one of the characters in the drama known as Kierkegaard's authorship, and who can only by a leap be identified with SÅK. Perhaps what the character S. Kierkegaard illustrates is how dedication to the religious sucks all of the dialectical sap from a human being, making him fit only for caricature.

[14]A distinction can be made here. It has already been made (for example, by Kant in *SdF*: 37). A thing can be rational in itself, κατ αυτον, or it can be rational for us, κατ ανθροπον. For the

purpose of this project that distinction is ruled out of bounds since Kant and Kierkegaard agree that reason as human beings have it is reason (Kant), or at least is all we can ever know of it (Kierkegaard). It is self-evident that if rational κατ αυτον exceeds rational κατ ανθροπον we can only identify them, as Kant does, if ανθροποσ ανθροποι δαιμονιον. It is also self-evident that if the rational κατ αυτον exceeds the rational κατ ανθροπον we would have no way of knowing it. The medievals who used this distinction did not know that κατ αυτον rationality exceeded κατ ανθροπον rationality. They believed it. Their faith has exactly the same form as informs S. Kierkegaard's discourses: believing God, believing in God, believing that God. (Cf. for example, Thomas Aquinas, *Summa Theologica* II-II, Q.2, a.2, who says that faith believes God, believes in a God, believes in God. Though the phrasing of the last two is different from Kierkegaard's, the point is the same.)

[15]Whether we call X God-Man, or just God who reveals himself (speaks) as the infinitely different to human beings makes no difference. Cf. the end of this chapter; also Kant's *Religion* and the arguments which were rehearsed in Chapter 2. Kant stands against both Incarnation and Revelation for the same reason: the absolutely different cannot become absolutely alike.

[16]Whether or not it ever was possible is not a timely question. Anti-Climacus clearly thinks that Aristotle, Socrates, and paganism in general were in error by their own fault. That seems unreasonable and offensive. It is unreasonable and offensive.

[17]In these democratic and relativistic days, when every man's opinion is as good as every other man's, it is considered

undemocratic (that is the highest insult—one would not, these days, want to say "wrong") to hold such a position. Nonetheless Kierkegaard and Kant, among others, held such a position. If the unexamined life is not worth living, then some people's opinions about the nature of their lives is not accepted as good money. Philosophers (people who hold that the unexamined life is not worth living, implying that every opinion is not created equal) hold the position they do because they think some things are true about human beings and their lives. They may be undemocratic for that. One could not, these days, say that they are wrong. Anti-Climacus calls this undemocratic effect the opinionativeness of the truth (*SUD*: 175).

[18]Perhaps I am mistaken. Perhaps it was not the title. He confesses: "Vainly I have tried to make myself believe that if the face of the book had not been turned up, and if the strange title had not tempted me, I should not have fallen into temptation, or I should at least have resisted it. [But then he immediately takes that confession back:] The title was peculiar, not so much in itself as because of its surroundings" (*E/Or* I: 299). He protests again: "The title of the book did not strike me in itself. [And then gives back the confession:] ... I do not deny, after that first glimpse, that the title was selected with much taste and understanding, with a true, aesthetically objective superiority over himself and over the situation. The title harmonizes perfectly with the whole content of the diary" (300).

[19]He would be "the spirit of sensuality"—a demon. He would be *Don Giovanni* (who can only appear as wordless music). Cf. *E/Or* I: "The Immediate Stages of the Erotic or The Musical Erotic."

[20]Someone I've read made up this excuse—"if this isn't a word, it should be." "Misanthropic" is too general a passion for what Cordelia is feeling. Doesn't it seem strange that we have a word like "misogyny," but no word on the other side? So then, in the interests of fairness—misvironic. Johannes is on the verge of coining this term himself when he says, in the entry after the seduction, that Cordelia should, at this point, be turned into a man (*E/Or* I: 440).

[21]Bertrand Russell, "A Free Man's Worship," in *Mysticism and Logic*, (1902): 47-48. One thing can be said for Lord Russell: he may not be logically clear, but he's honest. Sheerly by accident the computer printed this out in verse in one rough draft. I thought it was very creative and have tried to keep it just as the computer first suggested, it has been quite a challenge, as the other computers have tried to standardize it and turn it into prose.

[22]T.S. Eliot, "Murder in the Cathedral, *Complete Poems and Plays*, 1909-1950, New York: Harcourt, Brace and World (1971): 192ff.

[23]Since we begin by assuming the truth of the Paradox— J.C.'s poetic name for a contradiction—a logician will not be surprised if we succeed in proving all the implications we wish to prove.

[24]Louis Mackey was, at one time, fond of asking me why Anti-Climacus opposes faith, not hope, to despair, since *despero* and *spero* are such direct opposites in Latin—a language in which Kierkegaard was fluent. He has since given up asking me, which I suppose means that I missed the point. I did that frequently. Be that as it may, he suggests that this opposition may be due to the fact that in Danish despair (*Fortvivlelse*) is an intensification of doubt

(*Tvivl*) and so faith is a more natural opposition to doubt than hope is. This structural relationship certainly goes quite well with Climacus' definition that "an objective uncertainty held fast in an appropriation-process of the most passionate inwardness is the truth ... [and that] that definition of truth is an equivalent expression for faith" (*CUPS*: 182). Faith, then, contains doubt (*Tvivl*) as a mastered moment and so despair (*Fortvivlese*) has no entry. But if faith is directly opposed to despair then hope is directly a sign of faith. Faith believes in God (who is that all things are possible) and that God makes good. Hope for oneself expects that good for oneself; hope for others expects it for them. Therefore by giving up on one's neighbor one has limited what it is possible for God to do. But to limit God is no longer to believe God, but to believe one's own reason. It is interesting to note that Kierkegaard says (after Regina marries Schlegel) "if I had had more faith, I would have married Regina." His loss of hope that he could both marry and be a religious author is concomitant with a lack of faith: Her absence is the sign of his lack.

[25]It is also not accidental that S. Kierkegaard chose for his title a word used in the title of another book: *Apostlenes Gjerninger*, <u>Acts</u> *of the Apostles*.

Notes to Conclusion

[1]Alan Donagan, in *The Theory of Morality*, Chicago: University Press (1977), claims that a moral theory ought to be able to avoid moral problems *simpliciter*, but it is no argument against a moral theory if it cannot resolve moral problems *secundum quid* (145). What if all of our moral problems are *secundum quid*?

[2]Louis Mackey, *Kierkegaard: A Kind of Poet*, 285

[3]Kierkegaard appended to his dissertation, *On the Concept of Irony, with Constant Reference to Socrates,* 15 theses to be defended orally. As an appendix they were extraneous to the text of the dissertation, these theses are placed as a conclusion because they are not extraneous. Nor is this a dissertation.

BIBLIOGRAPHY

Works by Kant

References to the works of Kant are noted by abbreviations within the text. Pagination is according to the *Akademie Ausgabe*, except for *Rel*, which is according to the standard English translation.

Conflict of the Faculties, (*SdF*). Translated by Mary Jane Gregor. New York: Abaris Books, 1979.

Critique of Judgement, (*KU*). Translated by James Creed Meredith. Oxford: Clarendon Press, 1952.

Critique of Practical Reason, (*KPV*). Translated by Lewis White Beck. Indianapolis: Bobbs-Merrill, 1956.

Critique of Pure Reason, (A.../B...). Translated by Norman Kemp Smith. London: St. Martin's Press, 1970.

Doctrine of Virtue, (*DV*). Translated by Mary Jane Gregor. Philadelphia: University of Pennsylvania Press, 1964.

Education, (*Ed*). Translated by Annette Churton. Ann Arbor: University of Michigan Press, 1960.

"The End of All Things," (*End*). Translated by Ted Humphrey in *Perpetual Peace and Other Essays*. Indianapolis: Hackett, 1983.

Foundations of the Metaphysics of Morals, (*FMM*). Translated by Lewis White Beck. Indianapolis: Bobbs-Merrill, 1959.

The Kant-Eberhard Controversy, (*KE*). Translated by Henry E. Allison. Baltimore: Johns Hopkins Press, 1973.

Kant: Philosophical Correspondence 1759-99, (*Letters*, date and person). Translated and edited by Arnulf Zweig. Chicago: University Press, 1967.

Metaphysical Elements of Justice, (*EJ*). Translated by John Ladd. Indianapolis: Bobbs-Merrill, 1965.

On the Old Saying: That May Work in Theory, but Not in Practice, (*TP*). Translated by E. B. Ashton. Philadelphia: University of Pennsylvania Press, 1974.

The One Possible Basis for a Demonstration of the Existence of God, (*EG*). Translated by Gordon Treash. New York: Abaris Books, 1979.

Perpetual Peace, (*PP*). Translated by M. Campbell Smith. New York: Library of the Liberal Arts, 1948.

Prolegomena to Any Future Metaphysics, (*Pro*). Translated by Lewis White Beck. Indianapolis: Bobbs-Merrill, 1950.

Religion Within the Limits of Reason Alone, (*Rel*). Translated by Theodore M. Greene and Hoyt H. Hudson, with and introductory essay by John Silber. New York: Harper and Row, 1960.

What is Enlightenment?, (*E*). Translated by Louis Infield. New York: Harper and Row, 1963.

Works By Kierkegaard

References to the works of Kierkegaard are noted by abbreviations within the text. Pagination is according to the listed English translation. I have sometimes changed the translation slightly without noting it in the text.

On Authority and Revelation, (*AR*). Translated by Walter Lowrie. New York: Harper Torchbooks, 1966.

Christian Discourses, (*XD*). Translated by Walter Lowrie. Princeton: University Press, 1974.

The Concept of Anxiety, (*CA*). Translated by Reidar Thomte with Albert B. Anderson. Princeton: University Press, 1980.

The Concept of Irony, (*Irony*). Translated by Lee M. Capel. Bloomington: Indiana University Press, 1965.

Concluding Unscientific Postscript, (*CUPS*). Translated by David F. Swenson and Walter Lowrie. Princeton: University Press, 1941.

Johannes Climacus or, De Omnibus Dubitandum Est (*DODE*). Translated by T. H. Croxall. Stanford: University Press, 1958.

Edifying Discourses, *(ED)*. Translated by David F. and Lillian Marvin Swenson. New York: Harper Torchbooks, 1958.

Either / Or Volume I, *(E / Or* I). Translated by David F. and Lillian Marvin Swenson. Princeton: University Press, 1959.

Either / Or, Volume II, *(E / Or* II). Translated by Walter Lowrie. Princeton: University Press, 1959.

Fear and Trembling, *(FT)*. Translated by Howard V. and Edna H. Hong. Princeton: University Press, 1983.

Papirer, *(P*, Volume number). Udgivne af P. A. Heiberg og V. Kuhr. København: Gyldendal, 1909-1920. The translations are mine.

Philosophical Fragments, *(PF)*. Translated by Howard V. and Edna H. Hong. Princeton: University Press, 1985.

The Point of View for My Work as an Author, *(PV)*. Translated by Walter Lowrie. Edited by Benjamin Nelson. New York: Harper Torchbooks, 1962.

Prefaces: Light Reading for Certain Classes as the Occasion May Require *(Prefaces)*. Translated and introduced by William McDonald. Tallahassee: Florida State University Press, 1989.

Repetition, *(Rep)*. Translated by Howard V. and Edna H. Hong. Princeton: University Press, 1983.

Samlede Værker, *(SV*, Volume number). Udgivne af A. B. Drachmann, J. L. Heiberg, og H. O. Lange. København: Gyldendal, 1901-1906.

The Sickness Unto Death, *(SUD)*. Translated by Walter Lowrie. Princeton: University Press, 1954.

Training in Christianity, *(TC)*. Translated by Walter Lowrie. Princeton: University Press, 1967.

Works of Love, *(WL)*. Translated by Howard Hong. New York: Harper Torchbooks, 1962.

Secondary Sources on Kant

Albrecht, Michael. ""Gluckseligheit aus Freiheit" und "empirische Gluckseligheit:" Eine Stellungsnahme" in *Akten des 4. Internationalen Kant-Kongressus,* Teil II.2: 563-567. Berlin: Walter de Gruyter, 1974.

Beck, Lewis White. *A Commentary on Kant's* Critique of Practical Reason Chicago: University Press, 1960.

Bennett, Jonathan. "Commentary on Kant's Theory of Freedom" in *Self and Nature in Kant's Philosophy*. Edited by Allan W. Wood. Ithaca: Cornell University Press (1984): 102-112.

Deleuze, Gilles. *Kant's Critical Philosophy: The Doctrine of the Faculties*. Translated by Hugh Tomlinson and Barbara Habberjam. Minneapolis: University of Minnesota Press, 1984.

Engelhardt, H. Tristram. "Kantian Knowledge of Other Persons— An Exploration" in *Akten des 4. Internationalen Kant-Kongressus* Teil II.2: 576-781. Berlin: Walter de Gruyter, 1974.

Heidegger, Martin. *Kant and the Problem of Metaphysics*. Translated by James S. Churchill. Bloomington: Indiana University Press, 1962.

Kroner, Richard. *Kant's Weltanschauung*. Translated by John E. Smith. Chicago: University Press, 1956.

Paton, H. J. *The Moral Imperative.* New York: Harper and Row, 1965.

_____. *Kant's Metaphysics of Experience.* New York: Humanities Press, 1970.

Pieretti, Antonio. "The Reich der Zwecke as Possible Foundation of Personal Intersubjectivity" in *Akten des 4. Internationalen Kant-Kongressus,* Teil II.2: 582-589. Berlin: Walter de Gruyter, 1974.

Rotenstreich, Nathan. "Happiness and the Primacy of Practical Reason" in *Akten des 4. Internationalen Kant-Kongressus*, Teil III: 103-123. Berlin: Walter de Gruyter, 1974.

Shell, Susan Meld. *The Rights of Reason: A study of Kant's philosophy and politics*. Toronto: University Press, 1980.

Wick, Warner. "Truth's Debt To Freedom." *Mind* 73 (1964): 527-537.

Wood, Allen W. *Kant's Moral Religion*. Ithaca: Cornell University Press, 1970.

Secondary Sources on Kierkegaard

Agacinski, Sylviane. *Aparté: Conceptions and Deaths of Søren Kierkegaard*. Translated by Kevin Newmark. Tallahassee: Florida State University Press, 1988.

Fendt, Gene. *Works of Love?: Reflections on Works of Love*. Potomac, Md: Scripta Humanistica, 1990.

Lowrie, Walter. *Kierkegaard*. New York: Oxford University Press, 1938.

Mackey, Louis. *Kierkegaard: A Kind of Poet*. Philadelphia: University of Pennsylvania Press, 1971.

_____. *Points of View: Readings of Kierkegaard*. Tallahassee: Florida State University Press, 1986.

Meyer, Raphael. *Forlovelsen*. Udgivne for Fru Regine Schlegel. Kjøbenhavn: Gyldendal, 1904.

Nielsen, Harry A. *Where the Passion Is: A Reading Of Kierkegaard's* Philosophical Fragments. Tallahassee: Florida State University Press,1983.

Smyth, John Vignaux. *A Question of Eros: Irony in Sterne, Kierkegaard and Barthes*. Tallahassee: Florida State University Press, 1986.

Taylor, Mark C. *Journeys to Selfhood: Hegel and Kierkegaard*. Berkeley: University of California Press, 1971.

Walker, Jeremy. *To Will One Thing*. Montreal: McGill-Queens University Press, 1972.

Other Sources

Aquinas, Thomas. *Summa Theologica*. Translated by the Fathers of the English Dominican Province. New York: Benziger Brothers, 1947.

Aristotle. *De Anima*. Translated by J. A. Smith in <u>Basic Works of Aristotle.</u> Edited by Richard McKeon. New York: Random House, 1941.

_____. *Physics*. Translated by R. P. Hardie and R. K. Gaye, in <u>Basic Works of Aristotle.</u> Edited by Richard McKeon. New York: Random House, 1941.

_____. *Poetics*. Translated by Ingram Bywater in <u>Basic Works of Aristotle.</u> Edited by Richard McKeon. New York: Random House, 1941.

_____. *Rhetoric*. Translated by Rhys Roberts in <u>Basic Works of Aristotle.</u> Edited by Richard McKeon. New York: Random House, 1941.

Arnold, Matthew. "Dover Beach," in *Victorian Poetry and Poetics*, 2nd ed. Edited by Walter E. Houghton and G. Robert Stange. Boston: Houghton-Mifflin Co., 1968.

Augustine. *Confessions*. Translated by John K. Ryan. Garden City, New York: Doubleday-Image, 1960.

_____. *On Christian Doctrine*. Translated by D. W. Robertson, Jr. Indianapolis: Bobbs-Merrill, 1958.

_____. *De Trinitate, (DT)* Translated by Stephen McKenna, C.SS.R. Washington: Catholic University Press, 1963.

Ayer, A. J. *Language, Truth and Logic*. New York: Dover Press, 1952.

Barthes, Roland. *A Lover's Discourse: Fragments*. Translated by Richard Howard. New York: Hill and Wang, 1978.

_____. "Authors and Writers," in *A Barthes Reader*. Edited by Susan Sontag. New York: Hill and Wang (1982): 185-193.

_____. "From Work to Text," in *Textual Strategies: Perspectives in Post-Structural Criticism*. Edited by Josue V. Harari. Ithaca: Cornell University Press (1979): 73-81.

_____. "Myth Today," in *A Barthes Reader*. Edited by Susan Sontag. New York: Hill and Wang (1982): 185-193.

Camus, Albert. "Absurd Creation," in *The Myth of Sisyphus and Other Essays*. Translated by Justin O' Brien. New York: Vintage Press, 1955: 69-87.

Caputo, John. *Radical Hermeneutics*. Bloomington, Indiana: University Press, 1987.

_____. "Telling Left from Right: Hermeneutics, Deconstruction, and the Work of Art," *Journal of Philosophy* 83 (1986): 678-685.

Derrida, Jacques. "The time of a thesis: punctuations," in *Recent French Philosophy*. Cambridge: University Press.

Descartes, Rene. *Meditations on the First Philosophy*. Translated by F. E. Sutcliffe. Baltimore: Penguin Books, 1968.

Donagan, Alan. *The Theory of Morality*. Chicago: University Press, 1977.

Dostoyevsky, Fyodor. *The Brothers Karamazov*. Translated by Constance Garnett. New York: Random House Modern Library, no copyright date.

Eliot, T. S. *The Complete Poems and Plays: 1909-1950* . New York: Harcourt, Brace and World, 1971.

Foucault, Michel. "What Is an Author?" in *Textual Strategies: Perspectives in Post-Structural Criticism.* Edited by Josue V. Harari. Ithaca: Cornell University Press (1979): 141-160.

Frye, Northrop. *Anatomy of Criticism: Four Essays.* Princeton: University Press, 1957.

Gewirth, Alan. *Reason and Morality.* Chicago: University Press, 1978.

Hare, R. M. "The University Discussion," in *Readings in the Philosophy of Religion.* Edited by Baruch Brody. Englewood Cliffs, New Jersey: Prentice-Hall, 1974.

Hegel, G. F. W. *Phenomenology of Spirit.* Translated by A. V. Miller. Oxford: University Press, 1977.

Hix, Harvey. "What part ob yu iz deh poEM? Authorship and Authority in Interpretation." Doctoral Dissertation, The University of Texas, 1987.

Hopkins, G. M. "The Wreck of the Deutschland," in *Victorian Poetry and Poetics*, 2nd ed. Edited by Walter E. Houghton and G. Robert Stange. Boston: Houghton-Mifflin Co., 1968.

Murdoch, Iris. *The Sovereignty of Good.* New York: Routledge and Kegan Paul (ARK), 1985.

Nehemas, Alexander. "What an Author Is." *Journal of Philosophy* LXXXIII (1986): 685-691.

Orwell, George. *1984.* New York: Harcourt, Brace and World, 1949.

Plato. *Meno.* Translated by W. K. C. Guthrie in The Collected Dialogues of Plato. Edited by Edith Hamilton and Huntington Cairns. Princeton: University Press, 1961.

_____. *Republic.* Translated by Paul Shorey in The Collected Dialogues of Plato. Edited by Edith Hamilton and Huntington Cairns. Princeton: University Press, 1961.

_____. *Symposium*. Translated by Michael Joyce in <u>The Collected Dialogues of Plato</u>. Edited by Edith Hamilton and Huntington Cairns. Princeton: University Press, 1961.

Rilke, Rainer Maria. *Duino Elegies*. With a translation by C. F. MacIntyre. Berkeley: University of California Press, 1961.

Russell, Bertrand. "A Free Man's Worship," in *Mysticism and Logic and Other Essays*. 39 Paternoster Row, London: Longmans, Green and Company, (1918): 46-57.

Shakespeare, William. *The Complete Works* General editor Alfred Harbage. New York: Viking Press, 1969. Plays noted by standard abbreviation in text. Sonnets by number in text.

Silverman, Hugh J. "Authors of Works/Readings of Texts." *Journal of Philosophy* LXXXIII (1986): 691-693.

Tarski, Alfred. "The Semantic Conception of Truth and the Foundations of Semantics." *Journal of Philosophy and Phenomenological Research*, 4 (1944): 341-375.

Index

DATE DUE

HIGHSMITH   # 45220